Discover Your True Self

Discover Your True Self

Learn to Use Your Infinite Power of the True Self to Achieve Freedom and Happiness to Live the Life of Your Dreams

Nirmal Sharma, Ph.D.

All Rights Reserved. No portion of this book may be reproduced, stored in a retrieval system, or transmitted in any form or by any means- electronic, mechanical, photocopy, recording, scanning, or other-except for brief quotations in critical reviews or articles without the prior permission of the author.

Published by Game Changer Publishing

ISBN: 978-1-7370407-3-6

www.PublishABestSellingBook.com

DOWNLOAD YOUR FREE GIFTS

Read This First

Just to say thanks for buying and reading my book, I would like to give you a 100% bonus gift for FREE, no strings attached!

To Download Now, Visit:
www.DiscoverYourTrueSelfBook.com/Freegift

Discover Your True Self

Learn to Use Your Infinite Power of the True Self to Achieve Freedom and Happiness to Live the Life of Your Dreams

Nirmal Sharma, Ph.D.

www.PublishABestSellingBook.com

DEDICATION

This book is dedicated to my family, Indira, Swati, Gopesh, and Anand for their continuous encouragement, dedication, love, and support.

**And to my teachers
Muniraj ji King of Silence
Mahavatar Haidakhan Babaji**

Preface

In 2015-2016 I was semi-retired in the Bay Area and asking for guidance and seeking to learn more about how I could help people. This is the guidance I received on writing this book.

- If you start - Focusing on positive, say something good, you can turn their behavior around
- Joy is the GPS of the inner voice
- Find out what you can enjoy
- What makes you come alive, celebrate, write and share your joy, make others happy, no blame, no shame, no complaint
- Write these books:
  Yatra- Journey of life
  Karma- Action for Joy
  Moksha- Freedom of Soul
  Living - In the world
- Write about maya, kaya, ancestors, yatra, moksha, antahkaran and karma. Keep others inspired by your visions, guidance, love.
- Invite people to experience God, Goddess, divine love, peace, and harmony, oneness, and write about Muniraj Ji King of Silence Babaji-God of love.

- Write about singing, peace, prosperity, abundance, mother divine Kali, why she is mad, how to make her happy, and prevent natural calamities, floods, wildfires, and earthquakes. How to live life as your true spiritual self.
  1. Daily practice for meditation in silence.
  2. Hear the Massage Divine is delivering every moment of every day.
  3. Turn to your non-analytical inner voice that comes from the source.
  4. Find a quiet place. God, what you and I are going to concentrate on today. The thing I need guidance in every day. How would you like me to serve?
  5. How can I live a life of my true spiritual self? Let the message come from the source. Keep Writing.

Listen to the intuition that speaks to your soul

1. Connect with your heart
2. Look for signs in the universe
3. Pay attention to your dream. Ask intuition to speak to you
4. Take time and write. What do you want me to do today?
5. What do you want me to know today?

Should I pay for the seminars and training? Yes, yes, yes. It's a small price to pay to become alive. Connect with others in joy, harmony, and love. Silently take in the energy from the sun. Be happy. Something good, very good, will happen soon. New job, new house, new car, new business will come, but first, enjoy being happy, give love, forgive all and yourself. Listen to your heart. That's where I live. I live in your heart.

Wisdom will come pouring out of you and action steps will become apparent!

Relax, love all, forgive and forget the past, create your own Golden future, Golden kingdom.

Write about it. Follow the guidance well and watch miracles unfold.

Ask yourself, "What is the guidance I am not following, not acting on?" Consciously and deliberately tap into inner wisdom. Write about Yatra journey of the soul where you are going.

Power of oneness and harmony
"We are all one with each other and with God" - **Babaji**

Let's work for peace criteria for our family and society, and not expect from God Buddha or the government to solve this problem. Humans have created this problem and now we are asking God to solve it. It is illogical. God would say solve it yourself because you created it in the first place. "We are one people." The problems we are facing today are due to minor differences in appearance, which is not real, only an illusion. Dalai Lama

Talk to me, your father, mother, lover, friend, and guide. I am always with you.

But first, be happy. Have no doubt you are loved, supported, guided every moment.

Start living a disciplined life of trust and gratitude. Love and serve all as if you are serving me. Write, write, and write about God. What have you learned by being devoted to me for 33 years?

By serving people with love, you are serving me. It's only me coming in form. Do good services, help others, be courageous, get up early, be happy, be joyful, be humble. Everything will come to you when you open your heart. Love your enemy, your children, your friends, your money. Everything will come back to you, love, money, family, and friends. Don't reject anyone. You are loved. You have all the skills, talent, peace, love, and joy.

There is a life force inside. Seek that. There is a gem. Seek that. How can I live as my true spiritual self?

Live as if you are God, Lord of the universe. Love all in the universe. Live with grace and love all unconditionally. Be happy no matter what. Be grateful to be alive.

Be happy you are here. Be a small child, a student, wanting to learn, teach, help, serve. I am always with you. You are not alone. You are healed. Whatever you will need will come to you. Now be God, be good, be a loving father, friend, lover, and creator of all. Money will come from investments, lectures, seminars, courses, and gifts from the divine.

Live here for now and when the time comes, you will be shown the heaven - the heaven on earth. Make this Heaven on Earth with love.

Life is a Journey. When it started, no one knew. The bible says that the beginning was the word and the Word became flesh and dwelt among us full of grace. We all are made of words or sound. In Hindu philosophy, that sound is called om. NASA recently discovered that om is the sound of the Sun. As one approaches the sun, you hear this audible humming sound of om, which sounds like the beginning of Hindu prayers chanting before any religious ceremony.

The journey of our life, of our soul, began million years ago when we separated our souls from God. We started our journey as a soul. God created us in his image so that he could play with someone like Krishna playing with his friends or playing with Gopis. This life is created for joy, to play and celebrate not to worry about expenses or living for money and dying without knowing who we are. We are all one with each other and God.

The modern world with information technology and mobile devices has become so complex that we have forgotten who we are, where we came from and where we want to go. Most people I know are worried about the job, having enough money in their retirement plan, and having multiple streams of income. We take on more on our plate and on our psyche than we can handle. Then we break down, have relationship issues, get ill and then we die. We keep working till our retirement age, hide the terminal illnesses from our own friends and family, and then declare that we have only a few weeks to live until we die.

We are on our own journey of self-disclosure. We find ourselves when we travel. The soul is one. There is only one soul that lives in all of us. In the beginning, there was only one that became many. We are that one eternal being that does not die. We have no beginning, no end. We simply take on different bodies when we are born to fulfill our desires and carry our karma from previous lives, millions of lives in different forms.

Once we came in contact with someone who has become eternal, Hindus call him Shiva, Christians call him the Holy Spirit. That is who we are. That is why Hindus have one father and one divine mother that have different names. She is all women and all knowledge. That's why the worship of feminine power began thousands of years ago. Also, male power is worshiped as Shiva. If we all are Shiva and Shakti or Sita Ram, why are we not joyful and have so much Suffering. The One who knows the truth of his own being treats everyone with love because there is only one of us.

Hindu poet and saint Tulsidas, who lived 500 years ago and attained self-realization, said to see all the world as Sita Ram, divine couple, because the whole world is penetrated and permeated with his and her presence. We are on this journey that started millions of years ago and have taken this body at this time to realize our oneness with God.

The journey of the soul or Yatra as it is called in sanskrit goes on until the soul becomes one with the infinite completely satisfied and does not want to play the game any more.

The Contentment of the soul is difficult as the soul is infinite all pervasive and can be only known through love and satisfied with love. That is how the devotion was born. You can only know him or yourself thru love. Only love can save your life–love is all there is. Love is God.

I was born in Varanasi, India, right in the middle of the most populated area, next to the holy Shiva temple of Kashi Vishwanath. To my left was a huge temple called Kailasa, which is where Shiva supposedly lived. To my right was a temple dedicated to the Saturn planet, who is worshiped as a blue god with large eyes and has hundreds of oil (mustard) lamps burning with black sesame seed. There are temples of Ganesha, Kala Bhairava, Hanuman and Radha Krishna right in my house and famous Annapurna temple where Sri Adi Shankaracharya had a dream of Annapurna the goddess of plenty and fulfillment who feeds everyone in Varanasi. True is a saying that no one goes hungry in Varanasi.

After growing up in such an environment where several hundred thousand people visit the temple each day from all over the world, I became very close to Shiva, Hanuman, and Kali Annapurna. All of them became my close friends as I saw them every day and several times a day. I asked them for favors which they granted me effortlessly.

In Varanasi, there is always Ramayana chanting going on somewhere, and they play it loud. So I got very fond of the famous saint Tulsidas who wrote Ramayana in Varanasi.

The reason for Tulsidas's enlightenment was his wife, who he was madly in love with and could not live without her. Once when she visited her parents, Tulsidas followed her at night and climbed into her bedroom when everyone was sleeping by grabbing a snake hanging from her balcony.

His wife said to him, "If you love God as much as you love this body made of flesh and bones your life will be a miraculous success." That is when he left her house and became a saint-poet. His most famous poem for liberation in the Kaliyuga is "Kaliyuga kewal naam adhara, Sumir Sumir nar Utare para."

In Kaliyuga only the name is your support, by simply remembering the name you can cross the ocean of the world and reach the other side.

So Tulsidas after being realized as having achieved self-realization gives a formula for completing the journey or yatra and realizing who you are. Just repeat "Ram-Ram" and you will find God or love is who you are. Ramayana is read all over the world by millions of people to achieve Peace, Prosperity, and Self-Realization. It is normally completed within 24 hours of continuous reading by a group of people who would sing it out loud. You can also read it quietly and feel this saint-poet Tulsidas Baba's love for "Ram."

The Wonderful name of Ram is so powerful that Hanuman can do impossible tasks like lifting a mountain, flying across the sea, and swallowing the sun by just repeating the name of Ram continuously for eons. There lies the mystery of doing the impossible task and the secret of discovering the infinite power of your true self Some of my favorite quotes from Ramayana to discover your true self are:

1. Ramhi Kewala Prem Piyara: Rama only likes love.
2. Jehi Janahi JInh tumhi JanaI: Only He knows you only to whom you reveal yourself.
3. Uma Kahahu main Anubhav apana, Sach hari nam jagat sab sapana: I tell you my experience. Only the name of Hari is real. The whole world is a dream.
4. Siya Ram Maya Sab jag jani: see the whole world as the unfolding of Sita Ram.
5. Ab Prabhu Krupa Karahu ahi Bhanti sab Taj bhajan karahu din rati: Have such mercy and grace on me my Lord that I always sing the holy names leaving all worries behind.

True self only likes love and reveals itself to you. If you sing the name of the Lord all the time, the whole world becomes a dream, and you discover your true self.

In this book I plan to introduce myself first, Then introduce the true self according to scriptures and other realized masters.

In the second half of the book, I talk about how to discover true self through various tools and techniques.

In our one-year program, "Discover Your true self," these tools and techniques are applied to remove the veil or the web of delusion covering the light of the true self. This is where the real evolution takes place as a lot of Karma from the past lives, from the ancestors and the planets are diffused.

It may be difficult or challenging to read the whole book in one sitting. It's better to read a sample or small chapter of the book, meditate on the words and reflect on the message of how it applies to your current evolution of the soul and discovery of your true self.

The higher the evolution of the soul the higher will be the degree of freedom and liberation you will experience. The higher joy and infinite bliss await you to meet your true self lying dormant within your own heart as the light of the true self enters your body, mind, and soul you will find more light in your body and you will be changing into a luminous being as the darkness is replaced with the immortal light of bliss, joy, compassion, and harmony.

I invite you to join me on the timeless journey of the soul and uncover the infinite possibility that discovery of the true self has to offer. In these times of great transition, get on the path of self-discovery and embrace the infinite power of the true self to live a dream life of abundance, happiness, and fulfilling relationships.

Table of Contents

Introduction 1

Chapter 1 - Who are you? 17

Chapter 2 - Letting go of fear 29

Chapter 3 - How to face obstacles 37

Chapter 4 - Transition of dark age to the golden age 45

Chapter 5 - Lessons from Ramayana & Mahabharata 59

Chapter 6 - We are light 73

Chapter 7 - DEVOTION - love yoga 79

Chapter 8 - Goddesses 91

Chapter 9 - Gods 103

Chapter 10 - Mantras rituals and meditations 127

Chapter 11 - Reprogramming the brain 149

Chapter 12 - Wake up latent dormant energies within 157

Introduction

My name is Nirmal Sharma. I am a Kashi Pandit or Brahmin priest and a scientist living in the USA since 1974. I was born in the East and educated in the West. I assimilated the best of both worlds while learning about my true self and living the American dream to raise my family in the USA. I was born in Varanasi or Kashi, the city of light and the oldest continuously living city in India, Right in front of the most famous golden Shiva temple of Kashi Vishwanath, the Lord of the Universe. My father's name was Chandi Guru, a renowned astrologer and my grandfather was a priest and a royal medicine man, Raj Vaidya. The love and devotion for God ran deep in my family lineage.

My father's formal name was Ram Chandra Sharma and my grandfather's name was Shyam Sundar Mishra. My grandmother's name was Radha Devi. My grandfather's favorite profession was to inspire people with his reading of Satyanarayan katha, the story of Lord Vishnu as truth, on the full moon or 11th day of waxing moon called Ekadashi at his followers' request. By simply listening to this tale of Vishnu, in which he appears in front of those who prayed to him with faith and simple worship, Vishnu fulfills all his devotee's desires.

He was given the house in front of the Kashi Vishwanath Temple at the very center of the holy city of light Kashi by one of his followers. In turn, he was supposed to perform daily worship at Radha Krishna temple located on the first floor of the house.

I grew up in that house assisting him with the daily rituals that needed to be performed. My grandmother had her own private home temple on the third floor facing Kashi Vishwanath Temple where she would worship several deities or small idols or statues of different gods every morning and evening. I grew up in an environment filled with spirit, energy, or Shakti with the sounds and vibration of Shiva or God in various forms.

Varanasi is older than history, older than Rome and Jerusalem. The city is home to thousands of temples, Sadhu's or ascetics and ordinary people from all walks of life seeking salvation or liberation of the soul from transmigration. It is believed that just by living in Benares, one gets liberated when they die. The Kashi Vishwanath Temple is one of the 12 Jyotirlingas or pillars of light, where Shiva appeared in ancient times. Haidakhan Babaji Mahavatar told Leonard Orr, an American devotee whom Babaji had given the name Makhan Singh Raja, Pujari of Madhuban and the founder of the Rebirthing movement, that Jesus had his first mundan or head-shaving ceremony in Banaras.

The Kashi Vishwanath Temple is visited by over 25,000 people every day. The Shiva Lingam is considered alive and worshiped five times a day with ritual bathing with five nectars called abhisheka with loud bells and drums with priests chanting in Sanskrit. The prayer has been handed down from ancient times by Saptarishis, the celestial beings who got the blessings from Shiva himself to promote his teachings.

The average pilgrims to the temple come from different parts of the world, traveling thousands of miles to get a glimpse or Darshan of the Lord of the universe just for a few minutes. The Darshan of the Kashi Vishwanath once would grant one liberation and one is transformed in one visit. The energy of the kashi Vishwanath or the Lord of the universe can be felt from a 50 mile radius as you approach Varanasi.

The temple is at the center of the city strategically placed and surrounded by 56 Vinayaka or ganesh temples and eight bhairavas and thousands of small temples in every street and alleys where vehicles are not allowed. Some streets are as narrow as three feet. Growing up in Varanasi in Vishwanath Gali is an experience that can not be described in words. You must experience it. The Lord entered my mind, body and soul every day, five times a day as the temple bells rang and the priests started singing loudly the praises to the Lord. The sound changed the DNA in every cell of my body. I am so grateful to the Lord for entering my mind, body, and soul once and dwelling there forever.

As I was growing up, I was completely fascinated by the temples all around me and I started reading the praises, mantras, slokas for Shiva and Parvati that are inscribed in Sanskrit on the walls of the temple. The first one is called Rudrastakam composed by a poet-saint named Tulsidas, author of the famous epic Ramayana read by millions every day. Rudra Ashtakam is eight couplets on achieving nirvana or liberation.

The first one goes like this:

"Namami shamisham nirvan rupam vibhum vyapsksm Brahma ved swarupam. Nijam nirgunam nirvikalpam niriham. chidakasha makash vasam bhajeham." I worship Lord Shiva who is nirvana or freedom and lives in the space of the heart and everywhere. He is neither born nor has any attributes.

Then in one of the couplets, Tulsidas claims that Shiva is "manobhut koti prabhasri Shariram." His body has the brilliance of millions of suns.

One of the prayers recited every evening says, "Asit Giri Samasya kajjalam Sindhu patre surtarvar Shaka Lekhani patramurgi Likhat yadi Giri'sya Sharada sarva Kalam tadapi tav Gunanam lekhparama na jati." Even if you make the ink using all the mountains and use the ocean as an ink pot and all the trees as a pen and have Sharda, the goddess of learning, write the greatness of Shiva, she will not be able to do it. The greatness of Shiva is beyond words. Once you realize that you are Shiva or Shiva dwells in your heart, your power is limitless.

There are other smaller temples within the royal court of Kashi Vishwanath. There is Nandi, the bull that he rides, Parvati, his consort and Annapurna, goddess of plenty that feeds everyone in Varanasi and the whole world. Adi Shankaracharya visited Annapurna temple and she appeared to him. He composed the Annapurna Stotram in praise of Annapurneshwari–the one who gives eternal bliss, Nityanandakari–one who gives the bliss of yoga or union with god, Yogananda Kari–one who destroys the enemies, Ripu Kshyaya Kari–one who strengthens the faith in dharma, Dharmarth Nishta Kari–gives the self-knowledge, gyan and vairagya or detachment. There are eight Kala Bhairava temples and famous sankat mochan Hanuman temple and 56 Ganesh or Vinayak temples surrounding the Kashi Vishwanath Temple in a 25-mile radius.

We also had our own temple of Radha Krishna on the first floor of our house facing the Kashi Vishwanath Temple that was open to the public for Darshan. The house itself was gifted to our grandfather so that he could take care of the temple and he was given a small stipend every month to look after the deity-like bathing them every morning and feeding them twice a day and doing the mandatory puja twice a day with an offering of lights and flowers. I was asked to take on this duty when I was 8 or 9 years old as the kitchen was on the third floor, and the deities had to be fed before anyone could eat or get the blessed food called Prasad. I still follow this ritual in my home every day.

As I grew up my family wanted me to be a doctor or engineer, not a priest. So I went to the local university BHU after high school and got a Bachelor's degree in Ceramic Engineering. As I was graduating, I saw an ad for a national scholarship for study abroad from the Government of India. The government would pay for you to study abroad, all expenses paid. I applied and got accepted. I attended the University of Illinois at Urbana-Champaign and got a master's as well as a doctorate in ceramic engineering. There was no problem getting a job. I got three job offers from Intel corporation in Silicon Valley. They flew me, first-class, to Santa Clara and sent movers to pack everything, including my trash can from Illinois.

The Intel job was very exciting as I was doing cutting-edge materials research on the ceramic parts used in the packaging of electronic circuits. There was a lot of wastage due to a lack of in-depth understanding of ceramic material. The challenge was the alpha rays emission from the package which we discovered was causing soft errors in the random access memories produced by Intel.

The technical problem solving was very satisfying, but I was having a lot of issues with authority and the confrontational work environment. In 1979-82 I attended an inner growth seminar in Palo Alto where I saw a picture of a young man with incredible radiance in his eyes. I was told that this was the picture of the ageless Mahavatar Babaji described in the autobiography of a yogi who had just appeared in a cave in the foothills of the Himalayas after a long time. His name was Haidakhan Wale Babaji named after the village of Haidakhan where he had appeared. I felt that this was the answer to my prayers. It is said in the *Autobiography of a Yogi* by Paramahansa Yogananda, if a man utters Babaji's name with reverence, he gets an instant blessing. There was so much magnetism, love, and compassion in his eyes that I wanted to see him in person. Moreover, I felt that I had known him in the past as a long-lost friend and wanted to be with him.

When I inquired how I could meet him, I was given the name of a resident in Redwood City, Toby Clark, who had been in contact with Babaji very recently and was the President of American Haidakhandi Samaj, the association of devotees who followed Haidakhan Babaji. I got in touch with Toby Clark who invited me to come to his house where they had a small gathering, singing and praying to Babaji.

Toby asked me why I wanted to go see Babaji. I told him that I happen to be from India and would like to see Babaji with my family, with my mother, and two younger brothers. He said I had to write to Babaji, and if I got his permission I can go visit him.

I wrote to Babaji and did not get an answer. I decided to go anyway because of the irresistible inner pull and the love I was feeling every time I thought about Babaji. Toby, his wife Cathleen, and I flew to India in

October of 1982 not knowing it was the Navratri festival. Toby was supposed to take me and my family to Haidakhan ashram which was in a remote village in the Himalayan foothills that were only accessible by foot or a horse ride. There are no roads to the ashram, and you have to cross the Gautama Ganga river seven times. When we landed in New Delhi, I was received by my mother and my two younger brothers. We were given the name of Dr. Arvind Lal who I was supposed to call to get further instructions on how to get to the Haidakhan ashram from New Delhi.

We were told by Dr. Lal that Babaji was not in the ashram. He was visiting a devotee in the city of Patna for a Navratri celebration, and no westerners were allowed. I told him I was not a westerner, only an Indian living in the west. I was given the address of Babaji in Patna. He said to ask any Riksha Wala in Patna where a Chandi Yagya was being performed, and he will take you there.

Toby, Cathleen, and my family decided to board the first available train to Patna. We could not get any reservations, so we decided to get in the third class where there were no pre assigned seats. Toby and Cathleen hopped in and found a safe spot in the luggage compartment and now I was leading them to see a Babaji I had never met. At the Patna train station, we asked a random RikshaWala to take us to the place where Babaji was conducting nine days of Chandi Yagya, and they did without asking any questions. When we arrived at the location of the Yagya there was a big banner with thousands of people in attendance due to the Navratri festival.

A young Nepali man named Surya Prakash came running and said that Babaji knew that we were coming, and he had made arrangements for us to stay and take a bath before Darshan in the evening. So we went to the place where the living arrangements were made. We took a bath with hot water that was prepared for us and rested. After rest, we went to the place Babaji was staying and got some flowers to offer Babaji. The Nepali boy came running again and said that Babaji was waiting for us. There were several hundred people gathered to see Babaji, and we could not get anywhere near him. The Nepali boy made a gesture to people to make a way for us. We were given a grand red carpet treatment where the crowd parted right in the middle to give us a path leading to Babaji sitting on a throne.

As we approached Babaji, my heart was pounding and my mother had a garland that she wanted to offer Babaji. My mother is only 5 ft tall, and Babaji was sitting on a throne that was beyond her reach. Babaji kneeled over from where he was sitting so my mother could put the flower mala or garland around his neck. I was grabbed by the people or Ganas or attendants next to him and started asking questions like do you live in Varanasi or USA, how did you get here, etc. Soon the Aarti to Babaji started, and people started singing loudly with drums and harmonium playing. I joined the singing as I could not stop myself, and Babaji started throwing Fruit Prasad at me that would hurt my stomach one after another like a little child playing. I was filled with ecstasy that I have never experienced beyond words, just pure joy and bliss. I was transported to the realm of bliss or Ananda Loka.

The next morning I was late getting up and when I went to see Babaji he was surrounded by hundreds of people singing. He was giving darshan with offering Fruit Prasad. I sat in the back while the music and singing were going on and could not stop crying. The tears came pouring out of nowhere. Then someone tapped me on the shoulder and said that Babaji is calling you and he wants to see you. I followed him to the front of the gathering where Babaji was sitting. I was asked to stand next to Babaji and fan him with a huge brush like a jig made to circulate air around him as he was giving Prasad or blessed food to the people who had lined up in a large queue to see him. Babaji started asking me questions as he was giving Prasad like how do I know Toby Clark, how often I saw him, how far he lives from me and several questions about my family in Varanasi. My mother was sitting in the front row several hundred feet away from me. When I later saw her, I wanted to tell her what Babaji said. She said she heard everything. Prakash, the Nepali boy, afterward told me how to do the pranayama and Japa and set up an Altar at home when I go back and do Aarti to Babaji twice a day at home. I am so grateful to Prakash and Babaji for continuing this practice to this day.

I went to visit Babaji several times at his ashram in Haidakhan in the foothills of the Himalayas between 1982 and 1984 while living in the Bay Area. I learned about Babaji through Leonard Orr, an American devotee's book on Physical Immortality. I had not met Leonard Orr in person, but I had written to him to which he had not responded. When I met Babaji he asked me if I was a follower of Leonard Orr. I said no, I was not his follower. I don't even know him. Of course Babaji knows everything. He didn't say anything. In 1982 one morning when I was visiting Haidakhan, I saw Babaji sitting next to a man I did not know. Babaji introduced me to him and said this is Leonard Orr you can ask him any question you want. Leonard Orr was not interested in speaking to me or getting to know me as he wanted to spend time with Babaji. Now Babaji had started speaking to Leonard Orr who started the rebirthing movement of connected breath to release past karma and taught rebirthing to over 10 million people. Babaji told me to ask him to jump from the fence they were sitting on. The hillside was very steep and Leonard had to jump at least 300 feet to obey his order. Leonard was not quite ready to take orders from me. Babaji asked me again why he did not jump. I told Leonard Orr in a very firm voice, "Babaji wants you to jump now." When Leonard Orr saw that he had no other choice, he started taking his shoes and socks off. Instead of jumping, he slowly started rock climbing down the hill, grabbing one rock after the other.

He finally made skimp when he was closer to the ground from a height of 30-50 feet. Babaji was forcing Leonard Orr to make conversation with me and showing him that it was his power and direction that was coming through me. After Leonard Orr made the jump, Babaji asked me to tell him that he was in pretty good shape, which I did. This pleased him, and he started talking to me.

Babaji arranged my marriage to my wife in1984 just before entering Mahasamadhi as I wanted a partner who would support my mission in life of serving others. Babaji said that since my case has gone to his court, he would arrange the wedding and write me a letter. He said, "chitthi likhenge." Babaji entered Mahasamadhi on Valentine's Day Feb 14th, 1984. I received a letter in the Bay Area a few days after his Mahasamadhi From Om Shanti, his secretary at the time.

The letter said the time and tide wait for no one. Babaji has arranged my wedding with the daughter of the Shukla family in Haldwani. I can get married on the Shivaratri day and enjoy the Shivaratri evening with other Babaji devotees. This is another way of Babaji blessing me with his grace and love on the Shivaratri when Shiva got married. The wedding ceremonies lasted all night and I stayed up all night to keep the vigil singing with other devotees from Herakhan. It is said that keeping vigil on the night of Shivaratri is equivalent to a million years of meditation.

The last time I saw Babaji was in December, 1983 in Herakhan where Christmas was celebrated. Babaji said that Jesus is busy on Christmas eve going here, there and where his devotees call on him. But he will be in Herakhan for half an hour on Christmas eve as Jesus was a student of Babaji and spent nine years with him in Tibet and Nepal. I had fun singing Christmas carols and a direct experience of the holy spirit and being with Jesus on Christmas eve in Herakhan on Christmas, 1983 the last Christmas Babaji spent in Herakhan. Just before midnight as Babaji left the huge Kirtan Hall-like tent that was set up for Christmas Eve he gave me a good look as I was singing the Christmas Carol and entered my heart with Jesus. From that moment, I have a strange yearning to be with Babaji and Christ every Christmas and sing Christmas carols no matter where I am in the world.

Babaji took his last trip to Allahabad in Late January, 1984 and established a Kali temple at the house of long time devotee Alok Banerjee. Babaji made a stop in Haldwani just before returning to the ashram. There was a gathering at a local devotee's house in Haldwani where my in-laws were present along with my brother in law Vinay Shukla, a long- time devotee of Babaji and the only rebirther in India. My mother-in-law was quietly praying to Babaji for her daughter's marriage. Babaji called my brother-in-law and asked him, " Is your sister married yet?" My brother-in-law said, "No Babaji, we are looking for a suitable match for her." Babaji told him to look no further. Get in the Ambassador car outside. The driver will take you and your father to Allahabad. There you take a taxi and go to Varanasi and give him my house address which was in front of the Kashi Vishwanath Temple.

Babaji told him that there you will find my mother and tell her that Babaji has arranged the marriage of his son with your sister.

My brother-in-law and father-in-law followed Babaji's order and hopped in the car. Upon arriving in Varanasi, they found out that my mother was not there so they took a bus to my mother's home where she was visiting her father. Upon arrival they declared that they are coming from Haldwani and Babaji has arranged the marriage of her son with their daughter. My mother could not say anything. All she said was when Babaji had already arranged the marriage, who am I to say anything? They went back to Herakhan and told Babaji that everything was set. Babaji had Om Shanti draft a letter and sent it to me on February 1st by regular mail, which I did not receive until February 15th. That's the Leela of Babaji around my marriage. He kept his word even though he had to take care of so many things in the universe before entering Mahasamadhi.

After I got married, one night my wife Indira had a dream that we were in Haidakhan Kirtan Hall singing in front of Babaji with many devotees. Babaji had a small baby in his hand. He tossed the baby up In the air and said, "This is a star, one who receives this will become a Siddha." The baby came down wearing a space robe and landed in my lap. Soon after that we had a baby girl. A star was born as my daughter Swati Sharma.

We have three children who follow Babaji's teachings and prayed with us every morning and evening when they were living with us. We created small home ashrams with daily morning and evening prayers, worship and meditation to feel the presence of God in our lives. We invited friends, relatives and neighbors to the fire ceremonies and created great communities everywhere we lived in Boston as well as Silicon Valley for the past 36 years.

I am writing this book for the following reasons:

1. To share my experience that led me to travel a less-traveled path of being in this world but not of the world.
2. To inspire and provide guidance to others.
3. To share a path and practice that led me to self-realization of my true nature.
4. To share the process of living in this world and find the light that shines within.
5. Help you discover the true self that lives in everyone's heart.

"The Lord provides His full protection to the devotee who totally surrenders to Him. Who can describe the joy of the blessed soul whom the Lord takes under his protection? He is moved by love not by selfish motive of the devotee. We should merge our will in His Divine Plan of Welfare to mankind and dedicate our life to Him with all our might." Param Guru Shri Mahendra Maharaj in Sri Divya Kathamrit.

Babaji taught us the mantra Om Namaha Shivaya that is more powerful than the atomic bomb. Everything can be achieved thru mantra, including victory over death. It can be given to anyone and everyone can repeat it all the time silently or out loud.

Babaji taught me simple Yagya to purify the environment to protect Mother Nature from climate changes and earth changes. Babaji is ageless. He appeared in 1970 in a cave in Haidakhan to tell people about the coming changes and warn people about kranti or revolution and transition of the Kali Yuga or dark age to the golden age. Every time there is a transition from one era to the next when the old ways of thinking and doing things don't work, a mass shift in collective consciousness is required. We need to evolve and realize who we are as a soul.

Shiva is the essence of your soul. In the golden age, the dharma is love and simplicity not hatred and jealousy. By simply practicing repeating the name of God the heart is purified, the hatred and jealousy is removed and God begins to dwell in the heart. How can God dwell in a heart that is full of hatred, envy and jealousy? When we purify our minds by meditation and start experiencing stillness and emptiness we can have love and compassion for one another. There are so many stories from Mahabharata I want to share when Krishna appeared on the earth plane to restore the dharma. Kaliyuga started after Krishna left his body.

If you want to be a winner in life you have to be on the right side of the dharma. What is dharma? In the great epic Ramayana poet-saint Tulsidas says that there is no dharma greater than helping others. There is no greater dharma than helping people who are less fortunate than you. Sharing what you have to help others Is dharma. The message from the last time a great shift in consciousness happened in the time of Rama the Avatar and Krishna is no matter how powerful you are or how wealthy you are, you will lose if you are on the side of Adharma giving pain and suffering to others. You can win by helping those in need and who are helpless. That is the last message I received in a letter from Babaji in 1984 before he entered Maha Samadhi. After Babaji entered Mahasamadhi or conscious exit of the body Muniraj ji which means the king of silence was appointed as Chairman of the Haidakhandi Samaj to lead his followers. Muniraj ji was a man of few words and led Babaji devotees in the west for 30 years. Upon leaving his body in India in

2012 he sent me a gift, a Parker pen and a dhoti which to me was a message to share my experience with Babaji and Muniraj ji for over 30 years through writing a book.

Sage Vyasa who composed Mahabharata and 18 Puranas was asked towards the end of his writing what is the message from all the writings you have done. His answer was helping others is the greatest of all Dharmas.

MY MISSION AND MY MESSAGE

My divine soul's mission is to serve humanity by the discovery of the true self and God realization.

My hope for you as you read this book is that you

* Get liberation and freedom by realizing your true nature and discovering your true self.

* Help you diffuse the illusion of death and realize the true self that is immortal, and live as long as you want in a disease-free body.

* Realize the purpose of the divine play in your life to understand and experience your oneness with each other and God.

* Realize you are God, and nothing is impossible.

* Stop all the suffering.

* You live in the world, but you are not of the world.

* Realize that everything we see is a great illusion, the goddess, none other than the Holy Spirit.

* Understand the mystery of the Goddess, who alone is the source of all power, wealth and intelligence.

* To gain a miraculous Life and supernormal powers by using the ancient secrets of wisdom tradition.

* Know who you are and go beyond the mind's programming. Take a deep dive within to tap into your true self.

* Remove the programming on DNA level by the society, the media and stop spending way too much time thinking about yesterday, tomorrow and what you don't have.

* Stop thinking about others and spend enough time discovering yourself: the supreme joy through meditation and company of other like-minded people.

CHAPTER 1

Who are you?

*"I am the witness separate of all
I am pure consciousness
I am the eternal Shiva
I was not born
I have neither body, nor senses, nor mind
I the supreme self dwell in the Lotus of the heart
I am pure
I am one without a second "*

~ Kaivalya Upanishad

We are one with each other and God. We are not our body, not our mind. We are one immortal soul. We are God; we are eternal. That's who you are. Basically, I am you, Babaji of Haidakhan, Mahavatar Babaji is the most realized, ageless eternal being that I have met. He says I am you. I am nobody; I'm just a mirror in which you can see yourself. At the same time, he says, I am closer to you than you think. I'm everywhere. Basically, I'm everything. No matter who you are, you are everything. You're one with me. That means I am the creator. I am God, or I am Shiva. Who we are is an eternal soul, an immortal soul that does not perish, that does not die. Krishna says in Bhagavad Gita, "Nainam,

Kshindam Shastrani, Nainam dahati pavakah." Meaning: There is no weapon made to pierce this soul, and even the fire cannot burn it. Water cannot wet it. Because you are eternal, you are omnipresent. You are everywhere. You are like space. That's who you are, the universe infinite. You are like an infinite being, having a local experience.

Kabir Saheb or popularly known as Kabir Das, turned his body into the light and could not be found by his followers. Kabir Das was a 15th century poet and saint whose writings influenced India's Bhakti Movement. He is the other realized being, whose teachings I was very impressed by as a child. He lived in Varanasi, and there's a huge following of Kabir Das by a community called Kabir Panth. Millions of people still follow him today. He was born into a very poor family. His parents left him when he was born. He was picked up by a weaver family who raised him in a small village called Lahar Tara on the bank of the Ganges near Varanasi. He did not have a real mother and father. He was an orphan, but he wanted to know God; he wanted to find out and learn more about who he was.

Kashi or Varanasi is full of saints, realized beings, but nobody wanted to adopt him or take him on as his student because he was from a lower-class family. He went to the bank of the Ganges in the holy city of Varanasi in the early morning when it was still dark. There used to be a very famous saint living at that time. His name was Ramananda. He was the person who impressed young Kabir Das. Kabir Das wanted to be his disciple. Kabir Das knew the steps this holy man walked every morning to take a bath in the Ganga. He lay down on the steps of the ghat, which are the stairs leading to the water. When the saint stepped on him, he said, "Ram, Ram, Ram, Ram." These are the words that came out of his mouth. Young Kabir took that as a mantra because the words were coming out of a highly realized being who was himself, a god. Kabir Das started chanting *Ram, Ram, Ram, Ram, Ram*. He got the realization that he is also Ram. He is also just the word. Kabir Das has hundreds of books and poems that millions of followers chant every day through Kabir Panth. One of his famous poems is, "Moko Kahan dhunde bande Main to tere paas me. Na mandir me na masjid me, na kaba kailash me. Main to her sanso ki sans me." Meaning: Where you are searching for me, I am always very near you. I am not in the temple, not in the mosque. I am in the breath of every breath.

He also said, "Atma gyan bina sab sun. Kya kaba kya kashi." Without the knowledge of the soul, everything is dark and deserted, whether we live in Kaba or Kashi. Kaba is the holy place of Muslims. Of course, Kashi is the holy place of Hindus. I was very, very impressed by this Doha or couplet from a very young age. To me, the most important thing in life was to acquire self-knowledge or know who you are. Most people don't know who they are. The most important thing for you is to know your soul and realize how powerful you are. So, why are we talking about who you are, why we are spending so much time talking about who you are, because you are the universe, you are soul, you are eternal? You have no beginning, no end. You're never born. You'll never die. You were there before your birth, and you'll be there after your death. Everything else you see is an illusion, that is called self-realization, and people are spending all their life without realizing that. You probably heard about the self-realization fellowship, where I am, living right now very close to the Encinitas, California, self-realization fellowship that was started by a Yogananda in the West about 100 years ago. He was inspired by Mahavatar Babaji in India to come to the West and educate people in what's called soul science. The guru of Yogananda Sri

Yukteswar Giri wrote a book on soul science. The soul is everything, and you are everything.

The challenge is that we think we are the body, We are the mind, and we have limited power or limited capability because we relate ourselves to our body, too, with our mind. When you go beyond your mind, and when you have experience of the self then you know that you're unlimited. This is not the only birth you had, and then you realize your purpose why you come in here, and then you can achieve all your dreams because you are unlimited. Without spending too much time on this, we can say that there are a lot of people who have realized their oneness with God.

One of the very famous saints in India is Adi Shankaracharya. When he was only 14, somebody asked him, "Who are you?" He said "Chidananda Rupa Shivoham Shivoham." I am consciousness and bliss. I am Shiva. This is a very famous poem called Nirvana Astakam. "Chidananda Rupa Shivoham Shivoham." He says I am ananda or bliss, Eternal bliss. I'm Shiva. It is a long poem in Sanskrit, but he describes it too because he had an experience of the self. He says I don't have the illusion of death. I don't have any caste, or I don't belong to any community. I don't have a father. I don't have a mother. I don't have a birth. I don't have friends because I am eternal. I'm Shiva. I am Chidananda Rupa. I am consciousness and bliss.

This is who we are, but how do we get to the true self? What it requires is the control of the mind. When you go beyond the mind, then you feel the bliss because if you go within the mind, what you find is just thoughts and thoughts and thoughts and more thoughts. That's why we go to the mountain, go to the retreat or go to an ashram or monastery where there are no thoughts, no mind. Self has no mind, only ananda or bliss. People want privacy and want to live in the mountain, close to the water, because they want to feel The essence of the soul. That is ananda. That only exists inside of you. We talk about this further in the book. We have to go and seek the company of who is one with all fully realized or one who is not in a cage of the body.

What we have set ourselves up in is a very severe limitation like we are in prison, and we have our hands tied behind our back. Somebody who's already free, who has liberated himself can liberate you from your limitations. You need to find somebody, some teacher, some realized being who has realized that they're not the body, and they're not their mind, and they're not afraid to die. They know that there's no death. There's nothing like death. That's what we are looking for–that experience of limitless freedom. All the pursuit in life people want is to be happy, to be content. Basically, we're looking for that. Our true search is the contentment of this soul. When I met Babaji, he said, "Atm Tushti durlabh samsara." The satisfaction of the soul is very rare. You probably heard this song from Rolling Stones. I can't get no satisfaction. There's no satisfaction. It's because most people are extroverted. They look for the satisfaction outside contentment outside of themselves, with interrelationship and material acquisition or in entertainment or traveling or drinking, whatnot. But it's all inside of you.

The trick is how to turn inwards or go inside and have the experience of who you are, the eternal bliss nityananda so that you're not afraid to die. Just like Jesus, you're not afraid to go on the cross because, you know, nobody can kill you. Just like Krishna says in Bhagwad Geeta, "Nobody can kill you because it is impossible to kill the soul because the soul is like space. With no beginning and no end, you're everywhere."

How can you pierce the soul? How can you pierce the space? You're like the space inside a pitcher. When you break the pitcher, the space inside becomes one with this space outside, so you become one with all. There's a space inside the heart, and this space is also outside the heart. When you die, you become one with this space, and you basically become omnipresent. You're already omnipresent, but right now, you think you're limited within your body and your mind, but you are right now omniscient, and you are omnipotent. You are everywhere. You can do everything, and you can know everything. We can all know everything without knowing how it is in every one of us here and now. We can know everything here. Just like what is said in the Bible, "Be still and know that I'm God." So this is the secret of knowing yourself. But stillness does not come easy. If you find this stillness by killing or quitting your mind, it gives you incredible creativity. Your intuition opens up. Basically, you have a direct connection to God. All the knowledge is available at your fingertips because you can know everything. Now, whenever I have a difficult technical problem in my work and in my relationship, in my life, just by going within, just by tapping into intuition, I can find an answer.

That intuition is the inner voice. Some people call it the still small voice within. It's known as still as it is always there. How do you go inside, and how do you experience God? People spend their lifetime or many lifetimes trying different techniques or Sadhana. In self-realization fellowship, they meditate on the light that is in their heart, and they meditate on the breath. In Buddhism, they just focus on the breath. Buddha when he died. He told his son Rahul, just look at your breath. You just watch your breath. If you can just simply watch your breath the holy spirit, you will find God. You can see Buddha sitting in a statue, with his hands crossed and eyes closed, and his focus on his breath. The breath, if we just follow the breath, it will still your mind. Some people focus on the sound of the breath. Some people say a word like *Ram, Ram, Ram, Ram, Ram,* or some hold their breath while saying *Ram, Ram, Ram, Ram* to still the mind.

All the yoga is called "chitta vritti nirodha" in the yoga sutra of Patanjali. That means stopping the mind. That's what yoga is. Because you've already got that. You have a monkey mind. People are living in this day and age, having a mind that has 30, 40, 50 thoughts a minute. You're inundated with thoughts, and some people's minds are usually disturbed. That's when meditation with the breath is the simplest way to still and control the mind.

The next technique is the use of the word or sound. In the beginning, was the Word, and the Word became flesh and dwelt among us. The word or sound or mantra is another way to control the mind, still the mind and know the God within, know your soul. There are so many techniques that we cannot cover in the introduction. All the yogas are full of sadhanas or techniques to control the mind like the breath is one, and there are a lot of breathing techniques called pranayama that focus on controlling the breath. Krishna in Bhagavad Gita talks about merging inhale and exhale or prana and apana and vice versa. Leonard Orr, founder of the Rebirthing Movement, taught connected breathing techniques in which you take a deep breath in and let go of the exhale to more than ten million people worldwide. Then there are mantras that you can just repeat the same mantra over and over. Babaji Adries up arti says, "Japat nam bhava sindhu shushka ho." By repeating the name of the god, the worries of the world disappear and problems solved. The world outside is made up of just words. By just repeating one name of the God, *Om, Om, Om, Om, Om, Ram, Ram, Ram, Ram, Ram* whatever word you choose, you can still the mind.

Om Namaha Shivaya is the mantra that has been given to humanity for liberation, and you can achieve everything with this mantra, even victory over death. If you just say Om Namah Shivaya, Om Namah Shivaya, Om Namah Shivaya, Om Namah Shivaya, what happens? All the activity in the mind slowly, slowly, slowly ceases, and you become thoughtless. You go beyond your mind. Then you experience the stillness, experience the joy, you've experienced your true self. The first time I went to see Babaji, I had a lot of questions. I wanted to ask him, but when I went very close to him and tried to ask him a question, my mind became completely thoughtless- blank. I would forget whatever questions I had in mind. When you go to a realized being, guru, or saint who is totally still, totally thoughtless, and totally absorbed in his own radiance, love, and energy, you will find there you're very own true self. That's why we need the company of the saints who have been practicing the yoga or different techniques of Dhyana, Dharana, and Samadhi. It is only then you experience self-realization then you realize yourself, you realize God. "Sant Milan some Sukh kachu nahi." There is no happiness like meeting a saint. You are God. That is who *You* are. In order to realize that, you have to know yourself. The way you know yourself is to control the mind, be still and know that you are God. You have to learn how to be still, and then you'll find the God within you find the treasure. You find everything is inside of you, all the joy, everything you need. You'll become totally fulfilled and content in this very life. It is possible. That is what all the saints say, like Babaji, Sai Baba, Sai Ma, Shankaracharya, and also Ramana Maharishi, who used to live In the Southern part of India in a place Thiruvannamalai where there's a mountain. He called Arunachala mountain, the mountain of fire. He said that the mountain itself is still. When you go near that mountain, your mind becomes still. That's why Shiva is depicted in pictures living in the Himalayas because the Himalayas are like snow-clad mountains. When you just look at the picture of the Himalayas, your mind will become still because the Himalayas have been there for millions of years, covered with snow. It's just so quiet and so peaceful. Shiva is only a concept, but it's always shown as a being who is sitting on Mount Kailash. Kailash is his mountain, and that mountain is full of snow. There's nobody there, just that being one being, we'll say, sitting there with his legs crossed and with his eyes closed. If you imagine, if you just imagine for a minute that you are in the Himalayas in meditation, it's called Dhyan. That's how Shiva is available there. And know it is true. Through Meditation only, he is accessible through meditation or Dhyan gamya, ageless, deathless saint Babaji, and that is described in the *Autobiography of a Yogi* By Paramahansa Yogananda. He is there, here and everywhere.

I'm everywhere. You can only access me through love, through dhyan, by closing your eyes. If you look at snow cloud mountain Himalaya, the forever new immortal being sitting there for thousands of years, because he has been in meditation and on the mountain for thousands of years, since the beginning of time, you can imagine, if you can imagine such a being immediately, you'll be filled with, with the peace and light and most important thing is the love. Because who you are is the light that shines in the heart. Babaji says That I am Inside of you, I'm closer to you than you think. He is very far away, but at the same time, he is very close to you because he's everywhere.

So, this is the mystery of who you are. It is a great mystery. Most people don't even know how great they are because they are mesmerized by the media, by society, by their friends, by their parents. They just want to become like somebody, and they want to become something. But at the end of the life, when they get home, they realize they climbed the wrong mountain, and they were misled, and they don't find the joy or whatever they were looking for because it's not outside. It's already inside of you here and now. The whole purpose of life is to know who you are and you, What you are is ecstasy, joy, and incredible bliss. That needs to be realized because once you find that, then nothing needs to be attained because everything is already there, and everybody is after that. The millionaire wants to become a billionaire because they think once they have a billion, they will be happy. They will be able to do everything they want. By the time they get it, you'll have wasted your life, and they don't get the bliss because bliss is inside of you. Bliss is actually you. That's why it's called satchitananda. Buddha, when he was a young prince, was called Goutam Buddha. When he was young, he left his beautiful wife and the luxurious palace.

There's a book written in German by Harman Hayes a long time ago. He said that Gautama Buddha left his palace when he was a prince. He had a beautiful wife and a young child. When he ran out of his palace, he saw an old man, and he asked his guards that were escorts, "Who is this? Who is this man?" He had never seen an older man in his life.

The guards said, "You know, this is what happens to you when you get old. You're going to get old and die."

Gautama Buddha said, "What? I'm going to get old. I know that is not acceptable." Then that night, he went home and left his palace, his beautiful wife, and his young child because he went in search of his true self.

He said, "I want to find out why I'm going to die, why I cannot live forever." That's why Buddha left all the comfort, the palace, thousands of servants, maids, food, wine, everything to search for Nirvana. He went and sat under a tree. When he found his Nirvana and when he found the light within, he went to Banaras on the bank of the Ganges river, this place called Sarnath. He gave his first sermon. Buddha's teaching is also going deep within to find the answer. Buddha does not believe in God, but he did believe in finding the nirvana, stilling the mind and finding the true self within, and knowing who you are, and that is what everything is made up of. That's why it's important to know who you are. Once you know who you are, then you'll be filled with the joy that you have been searching for ages, not ages, but for eons. You'll find your mother, which some people call Amba.

Mahendra Maharaja, who spent his whole life in search of Babaji and finally made him appear in the human form, found the supreme joy within and wrote praise, "Amba ananda Rupa cha Atma Ahlad dayini. Apar Karuna bhava paramba nityam namamyaham." Amba mother of bliss, You fill me with supreme joy. Your mercy is endless. O mother, I forever bow to you. Inner supreme joy as the mother resides in the heart because it gives so much bliss and so much joy, and you'll be filled with this spirit or energy, Our Shakti, which is called the Holy Spirit. That's what the Holy Spirit is. You'll find that in India, they have given the Divine Mother different names. Amba, one of her names, means the mother of the universe. Basically, this is a sound, so that is the next step. Once you find out who you are, you are the word. Like the Bible says in the beginning, there was the word, and the Word became flesh and dwelt among us, So that's what you are.

CHAPTER 2

Letting go of fear

"The one without color appears by the manifold application of his power with many colors in his hidden purpose."

~ Shvetashvatara Upanishad

We all are one with each other and God, as I mentioned previously. There's only one unified field. There is only one controller, which we call God. In the beginning, there was a word that we call God, and the Word became flesh and dwelt among us. In the beginning, there was only one that became many. The confusion starts when you see the other as different from yourself. Basically, the other person is just an image of you, just like you. There is only you out there. It is an illusion that we are separate because in the beginning was the Brahma the Creator with whom was the word.

That means there was only one. There's no second. Eko Brahma dwitiyo nasti. There is one creator or the controller that we talked about of this unified field that everything is contained in. There's only one. We strive for that realization, that oneness with the Brahma controller. Then you can say, "aham brahmasmi" or I am God, or I am. I am the same in all of us.

If you want to be happy, then we have to really make other people happy. You become happy. One of the quotes I like from Babaji when I met him, he used to say, "when you're happy, I'm happy." When people ask him what he wants. He said, "I just want you to be happy. When you're happy, I'm happy. When you're at peace, I'm at peace."

There is a lot of fear and uncertainty, and insecurity in people's minds today because they're not sure about their future. There's a lot of enemies people have created, and the root cause of all that is we do not know that we are one with each other and with God. Once you realize that you are God, the next step is to see God in others.

Thousands of years ago in Bhagavad, Gita Krishna said, "Those who see me in all and all in me for him, I'm not lost, nor He's lost for me." So the people who love Krishna just see only him like Mother Teresa only saw Jesus in everybody she was treating. You only see your lover, or only see yourself. That is the place we want to get to because love is God, and God is love. The observer is observed. The observer determines what he is seeing. Beauty is in the eyes of the beholder.

The Bible says that he who dwells in love dwells in God and God in him. We are God. We are diluted by what's called Maya or illusion because there's only one. That one, you can call it the Word of God or Holy Spirit, that one without color appears by the manifold application of his power with the many colors in his hidden purpose.

There was Erhard Seminar Training (EST) in the sixties, and they talked about, "There's only you out there." Why don't we see only you, and the same thing it says in the Vedas that there's only one God and nothing else. Whichever way you look at it, there's only one of us. The reason we don't see that is because we don't go deep within ourselves. There are practices you can do to establish oneness with each other and God.

The simplest thing to do is to see yourself in all. You have to start practicing slowly, just see yourself in all, or see all in one whoever your mentor or your Messiah is. That's why the Messiahs don't have a name. They have names like Baba or Sai baba or Ananda because they have lost their identity. They have merged into that infinite one.

That is our goal, to merge into that one, that one spirit that lies at our heart and, the same spirit is in everyone that you see or you meet. So dining together, chanting together, singing together establishes oneness. Because all is love. "Love each other like I have loved you," that's what Jesus said. Babaji, before he was leaving his body, entered Maha samadhi and people were very sad and crying. He said, "I'm always with you and just love and serve others like you, love and serve me." This is the Maya that we're talking about.

We will go more in-depth on the practices and teachings from Yoga Vasistha, who was one of the greatest teachers of all times. He was teaching the avatar Rama, "Everything you see from birth to death is an illusion. Soul is immortal. It is neither born nor dies." The trick is to see that everything is made of energy. Everything is made of different colors, but they all originate from the same source and then eventually merge into that one source.

We don't realize this and we get into yours or mine, having a separation and conflict or animosity as adversity, all that can be eliminated by simply bringing light and love into your life. That is already given to you. That's why you have to have the company of a realized being or someone who practices oneness and shows you that life, how to live their life.

I've been fortunate to have a special relationship with Babaji and Jesus when Babaji was living in Herakhan from '82 to '84 and his successor Muniraj Ji for 30 years. Babaji was the teacher of Jesus who lived in Herakhan, a small village in the Himalayas from 1970 to 1984, but I was able to be with him toward the end of his appearance.

Babaji demonstrated how to live and how to love and how to treat people like you treat yourself. There's a saying in the Bible. There's a golden rule that says, treat others like you want to be treated. So for this just one rule that you follow or practice in your life and start seeing and thinking that we all are one with each other and God, there's only God, then, your life will transform dramatically, every conflict and resentment will disappear.

Your life will be full of miracles and of those around you. There's only a miracle every day. I see miracles which I never thought would be possible, and I cannot believe that things happen, that I'm still alive and talking to you and be able to talk about oneness.

So it's all the meditation practices that are changing the mindset and change in your perspective. It comes as you go deeper and deeper within your own self and start seeing the first distortions of your mind that you created, like a movie. Because you're the witness of that movie, when you start seeing a movie, then you can, after a while, start seeing the one who is watching the movie, and that is you. Slowly the movie stops, and then you are established in your own self. That is when you see the one unified field here, and then the only thing you see is God. Like Hanuman, he sees Rama and SITA Rama everywhere.

Ramayana is a great scripture that was written 500 years ago by saint-poet Tulsidas. One of the famous quotes from the Ramayana I learned as a child growing up in Varanasi was, "Siya Ram maya Sab jag Jani." See the whole world as Sita Ram, filled with the presence of Sita Ram because the whole universe is filled with divine energy.

When there is only one they called God, then you don't exist. There is a poem that goes, "Jab main tha tab Hari Nahi. Jab main hun hari nahi." When there is God or Hari I don't exist. When I exist, God disappears. "Ek Mayan main do sabak dekha suna na kan." There is a sword, and it goes into its case or sleeve. There can only be only one sword that goes into one cover. There's only one that can exist, either God or you. There's no room for two. You can either have me or mine or God. That is the key to finding oneness peace, a joy to only see God, and you are that, so is everyone else.

These are people who have realized that oneness and It's not that difficult. It just comes to you when he wants to be known when he wants to reveal himself. Who is he? He is your true self, or the God, who is inside of you. Tulsidas wrote the *Ramayana* 500 years ago because there was a lot of fighting going on between Hindus and Muslims, a lot of unrest like it is right now. He wrote this book called *Ramayana*, which is also called Ram Charit Manas. Basically, he described the character of Ram, the avatar, who lived on the planet earth. That was a long time ago, but we're living in a different age. Like some people say, Rama, lived a hundred thousand years ago.

There was a Ramayana written in Sanskrit by a sage called Valmiki. Valmiki means an anthill. Valmiki was meditating in the same spot for so long that his whole body was covered with ants and dirt. There were only two eyes that were open that he could see through. He just sat in one place because his guru told him to just sit in one place and say, Ram Ram till I come back. Don't move from here. He just sat there. Then he had the realization. He had the whole life of Rama The Avatar flashed in front of his eyes, then he wrote the scripture that is called Valmiki Ramayana, in Sanskrit, that was a long time ago, a thousand years. Sanskrit is a very difficult language to understand or even to speak.

Very few people or a very small percentage of people in India understand or read Sanskrit. Ramayana was created by Tulsidas in a local dialogue called avadhi so more people can easily understand. That's what Tulsidas did, and millions of people read this Ramayana or Ram charit manas every day. Some people in my family, my grandfather, and grandmother started the day by reading it first thing in the morning because it creates a great atmosphere in your home because there's so much love for God. Because he talks about the life of how God walked on this earth, they call him "Akhil koti Brahmand Nayak." He is the King of all galaxies, but he came down to earth because there was a curse on him that you will go down to the earth plane to live as a human being.

That's another long story, but the reason I'm talking about *Ramayana* here is that only when God wants to reveal himself can you know him. The exact words that he says in very famous lines are "jehi janahe jin tumahi janae janhi tumahi tumhi ho jai." Only he can know you to whom you want to reveal yourself. Once he knows you, he becomes you. Through devotion, a true love for God, you can discover your true self.

He shows the mystery. He shows himself, reveals his grandeur, his mystery, his light to you. Then you become him. You become God because God is no different than you. God is everywhere. He's in every cell of your body, in every atom. He's the vibration or the force that's everywhere in every living being, even non-living beings, animals, plants, five elements, stars, galaxies, everywhere. That's why it's important to see him only. There's only one, and that is him. If you keep yourself separate, then all the problems start. There it is, you have to lose yourself, surrender.

We all are one with each other and God, just know it, believe it, just have faith. Eventually, God will reveal to you. God is your soul. He lives in your heart. As you love and find a personal god called Ishwar in Sanskrit, somebody who loves you unconditionally, you'll become a little child, and then you'll be able to enter the kingdom of heaven. You will be able to see God in each other and then be able to create a heaven on earth.

CHAPTER 3

How to face obstacles

"Shri Mahaprabhuji wants a world of very brave and courageous people! With full faith and devotion to God and a firm determination if people follow the Path of Truth, Simplicity, and Love with Karma Yoga, they will reach their goal. When the whole world is burning with the fire of sins and sorrows and the flames are about to swallow the world, this is the only way by which humanity can be saved!"

~ Mahavatar Haidakhan Babaji

I referenced earlier in the book the Yoga Vashishta written by Vashishta, who was one of the greatest teachers who ever lived on the planet because he was teaching Rama, the avatar, about the Supreme self. He was telling Rama that when you're born as a human being, you forget who you are. Even when God comes down to earth, they don't remember themselves. I am quoting here from yoga Vashishta that, "The self is subtler than even space since it has no name and cannot be described, and neither the mind nor the senses can reach it or comprehend it. It is pure consciousness."

The entire universe exists in consciousness, even as a tree exists within a seed. One who says things that it is not more aware of its existence cannot be experienced indirectly just as the existence of camphor cannot be experienced by his fragrance. It alone is the self of all as consciousness, and it alone is the substance that makes the world appearance possible. This is from chapter three, verse 80 of *Vashista's Yoga*, which is a book you can get by Swami Venkatesananda, and the translation is almost 800 pages. I just quoted that from *Vasistha Yoga* that self is all there is, and you are the self, and everything else we see is what we call illusion or Maya because there's only one. You have to live your life, just like watching a play or a movie, so that you're not attached.

If somebody dies in the movie, you just walk away. You know, sometimes I watch a movie or a horror movie with my wife, and I don't like the feeling, and she says, "Oh, it's just a movie. They're just acting." But the whole life is a play. We are ageless, and the movie has no end. We just pass through life through our past karma, our desire, through our need to experience something. Some people call it unfinished business. We are here, but we don't need to get attached to an outcome or to a certain perception because death is an illusion, just like a drama. Because when you see, you realize that you have no beginning or end—you are. The self is the Shiva then even the illusion of death goes away because you are like his space. You're everywhere. How can this space die? So you just merge into this space by the grace and blessing of the one who has obtained the oneness with the Shiva or, or Mrityunjaya, or one who has victory over death. There are mantras you can do. "Om tryambakaṃ yajāmahe sugandhiṃ puṣṭi-vardhanam urvārukamiva bandhanān mṛtyor mukṣīya mā 'mṛtāt." That's the Mahamrityunjaya mantra.

We'll talk more about the mantra when we go into the chapter on ritual and mantra, but the mantras are the sounds that you can repeat that will give you the immortality consciousness of the soul or Shiva consciousness. The whole world is made of one indestructible soul, but we act as if we are going to die because that's what we have been taught. My mother, when she was 79 or 80 years old, said, "Oh, I want to go to India."

I said, "why?"

"Because," she said, "I want to die in India because everybody else in your family, your father and grandfather, died there, so that's the model they have."

They think that you have to get old and die, but the reality is something different. We are the eternal being living in a destructible or disposable body. You can also fill the body with the incredible energy of Shiva and remove all the disease which is there—so knowing that you are the creator that created, even this body. First, you were a little kid. Then you get old. It's just a huge change in the mindset, and this is not very far from the truth.

Most people just go from one life to the next or from birth to death, and they are born again and die again. Shankaracharya, the great sage we talked about, wrote a book called *Bhaja Govindam*. Govinda is the name of Krishna. Bhaja Means to sing it repeatedly all the time. Bhaja Govindam means just by singing the name of God, or remembering God, You can get out of the cycle of birth, death and rebirth. In that book, he said, "punrapi jannanam punarapi, marnam," that everybody is born again and then dies again. If you don't remember God or Govinda then you are trapped into the cycle of birth and rebirth. All you have to do is just remember Govinda, your soul all the time, and do your duty.

Then you will be free from birth and rebirth. This is the teaching of Krishna and Babaji. "You must remember me at all times and do your duty. If your mind and heart are set on me constantly, you will come to me. Never doubt this."

You turn off the monkey mind and know the self or God that does not die, the indestructible, that's everywhere. You have to develop a relationship, and you have to get to know Him, you have to get to know your own self, who you are, like Adi Shankaracharya who is considered the most enlightened being. He was around like 500 years ago. Shankaracharya says in that book, "punarapi jananam punarapi maranam." We are born again and again, and then we die, again and again, then we go into the mother's womb and sleep in the womb for nine months. If you don't want to be born again and die again, then you have to remember Govinda or God or your soul.

This is a long book with many, many chapters. I read the Bhaja Govindam a long time ago. There was a Vedanta teacher from India who used to come to Palo Alto, his name was Chinmayananda, and he established centers all over the world in South Africa, in San Jose, in Australia. He used to teach this book in a camp and went through each line word by word in great detail for many years. It was fascinating at first. When I heard him talk about Shankaracharya's Bhaja Govindam, it just stayed with me forever. Those words in Sanskrit have a power that resonates with you. If you hear something, it's like a song that will stay with you for the rest of your life. That's why "Bhaja Govindam," and "punarapi jananam punarapi maranam" are reminders to live consciously, so you don't have a birth, again and again, attain liberation or moksha. Most people who have been around Gurus have heard the word Moksha through the Guru Geeta mantra "Moksha mulam guru

Krupa" the root of liberation or moksha is Guru's grace. That's why you want to live as if this is your last life. A lot of people have a lot of desires, a lot of attachment, a lot of insecurity. They want to accumulate a lot of assets because they're afraid there's not going to be enough when they get old, and they won't be able to work.

But once you know who you are, then what happens? This tremendous amount of bliss follows you. You become one with God and whatever you want happens. It's thought manifestation because you are God who creates everything. When you become God, then you create everything simply by your thought whatever you want, whatever you think about will show up. You have to let go of the mind or ego, the sense of doership, and feel the bliss, and then you have to let go of what does not serve you and adopt an attitude of love and service.

One of the teachings that Babaji and Krishna taught in Bhagvat Geeta is called karma yoga. Karma yoga is not widely known in the West or practiced, but that's what people do every day from morning to evening. When you get up, you start working, you start making your coffee, brush your teeth, and then you take a shower, eat your breakfast, and then you go to work and check email or karma, just actions. Any activity in mind is karma. You cannot live without karma. Karma yoga is a Yoga for the modern age practiced and taught by Krishna in many chapters of Bhagavad Geeta. He says, "You do your work, but don't get attached to the fruit of action. The only right you have is to perform the action. You perform the action but do not get attached to the outcome."

Whether it is you want to make money or do your other duties in the world. I worked For 40 years in corporate America, in different ranks from a senior engineer to the engineering manager to Senior Director. I went in and did my work, Whatever I had to do, and forgot about the outcome. The outcome is not in your hand. The work is worship and your Karma Yoga is a great practice. What Krishna taught is the perfect yoga for this age, Kaliyuga. You do your work at the same time You repeat the name of God, remember God. "You remember God and do your duty in the end. You will come to me." That's the way we want to live, by practicing karma yoga in whatever you have to do while living in the world and offering your service to please others, thinking that they're God, without expecting anything in return.

There are many books that have been written on karma yoga. Karma means action, karma yoga means you do everything to unite with God. My wife gets up in the morning, and she starts working, working, working until she gets tired, and I'm sure it's a great service. At the same time, detaching from the fruit of action is karma yoga, don't get attached to certain outcomes, whether you are playing in the stock market or you go for a walk and exercise. You do everything you have to do, but don't expect a certain outcome. Whatever you get is fine. This is karma yoga, and it will give you liberation.

Babaji says to do karma Yoga or service that is good for the whole of humanity, something you do that affects a lot of people, and a lot of people benefit from it. Like building a hospital or building an orphanage or ashram temple where people can come together to pray. Babaji used to do a Yagya or fire ceremony where he would invite a lot of people, 300 and 400 people. It's a fire sacrifice. You worship the fire and offer bounties of the earth to the fire. It benefits the whole community as it purifies the environment and also burns the karma of all the people participating. That's how you change the karma of a lot of people. Karma yoga is a way to unite with God, serve God while you're living in the world. No matter what your role is, whether you're an engineer, doctor, or nurse, or janitor, you can provide service, and that service, you make it karma yoga by not getting attached to the fruit of your action. You are responsible only for offering your action as a service, not for the outcomes.

You do the best you can and offer the results to God and accept whatever you receive as your gift. That's the way to live in the world taught by Shri Krishna to humanity through his disciple Arjuna on the battlefield. It is the ideal way to live by offering your life to the divine that gives you liberation. It is like a mother who gets up in the morning and starts working at home, not expecting anything in return, whether it's cleaning, cooking, for the children, getting them ready for school. You can do the same thing whether you are a mother or father or brother and sister, no matter who you are. There are a lot of services.

If you establish a temple at home, then you can provide the same kind of service to the Devas, or divine beings that you establish in your temple, So you have a living presence in your own home. Karma yoga is a way to live in this world and offer your services doing acts of charity that benefit a lot of people. By serving others, we burn our own karma, and karma yoga is one way to not get attached to the fruit of our actions. Like if you're doing a charity and don't expect anything in return, and that's the hardest thing to do. By doing that, what happens? You free yourself from the past karma.

We all have lived countless lives, millions of lives, from the beginning of time. We have talked about changing our destiny, free ourselves from the past karma, which is done by service. Service to others is service to God. By serving humanity, you serve the Lord. The greatest thing you can do is to make others happy, and that's why it makes you happy. If you want to be happy in this world, think of everything as God. Everything is the Divine Mother, Holy spirit, and offer your services to them wherever they are, whether it's your family or your children are not.

In Sanatan Dharma from the beginning of time, this practice has been established like the worship of fire and the mantra, and in chanting, all have been documented in the Vedas. By following these practices, you establish the goddess in your body. What we're trying to do is remove the veil of Maya or illusion on our mind, body, and soul. By doing the service, by doing the selfless service, that's the most important thing. Selfless service means you give something expecting nothing in return. That's why you'll see, there're so many organizations engaged in providing service to millions, like in a third world country, there are a lot of homeless people, foster care, or hospitals. You find your own way of serving the people, serving humanity. This is the way to live if you want to be free from past karma.

If you have bad financial karma, you have done something bad financially in the past, then you cannot be successful in this life in the financial area. If you have bad relationship karma, then you will have problems in the relationships. If you have health karma, then you will have health problems. The way to get rid of that karma is you have to remove that karma and find a service that helps the people who need either financial help or a relationship or health type of service. Like we talked about hospitals, that's the way you can live in this current time. We have to look at how we're living and what changes we can make to the lives of others around us and make our life more enjoyable.

CHAPTER 4

Transition of dark age to the golden age

"To those that are constantly devoted and worship me with love, I give them the understanding by which they can come to me. Out of compassion for them, I, dwelling in their hearts, destroy with the shiny lamp of knowledge, the darkness born of ignorance."

~ Bhagavad Gita

Right now, we are transitioning from the dark age to the golden age, and there is a huge shift in the collective consciousness from a lower to a higher frequency consciousness. There is a lot of uncertainty about the future. There's a lot of fear in the people who have lost their jobs. People's relatives have died because of Corona. The massive shift in human consciousness is needed for a transition to the golden age. You can imagine we're going from a dark age to the golden age. We are going from darkness to light. What you're seeing, the fear, anger, violence is all darkness, but when you go to the light, it's love, joy, compassion, and bliss. This is a very important time that you should be grateful that we're living in such unprecedented times where we have the opportunity to evolve from a human to God. From a human being, you can become a divine being or God itself.

The one path that we talked about, karma yoga. Of course, you have to do your work, but it's a great opportunity to help others. That's one thing you can do, but also karma yoga is you do your work but do not expect anything in return. Everything is divine. Almost 5,000 years ago, in a time like this, on a battlefield, Krishna gave Direction to Arjuna, who was a warrior. He had incredible powers. When he saw that he had to fight his own relatives, his own family, his own teachers, he had to kill. He just lost his will to fight. Actually, he put his weapons down, and he said, I cannot do this. Please guide me. Then Krishna gave him the direction.

The Bhagvad Geeta has 18 chapters, and in each chapter, Krishna talks about how to live in turbulent times like now, in a war zone. Krishna, says, "**Those Constantly devoted and worship me with love. I give them the understanding by which they can come to me and out of compassion, I dwell in their hearts destroyed with the shining lamp of knowledge, the darkness born of out of ignorance.**"

Right now, everything is very painful, very chaotic, but it's all born out of ignorance. The Coronavirus itself is born out of massive congested negative energy. To face that bravely, you have to turn to God. You can become a devotee with a few months on this path. If you are faced with challenges in life, the one way to do so is to develop daily devotional practices that destroy the darkness born of ignorance. The fear is born out of ignorance. Love is letting go of fear.

Those who love God, God gives them abhaya daan, which means a boon of fearlessness. Fearlessness means you have no fear of death because you are immortal. The soul cannot be born, cannot die. You are indestructible, and that's another teaching from the Gita. Krishna told

Arjuna, what are you afraid of? Is everybody going to die? You're not the body, you're the soul, but these guys are on the wrong path. They're on the evil side, and they have to be destroyed. If you don't kill them, somebody else will. People die every day, but the soul lives forever.

You have to decide that if you want to identify yourself with your body that's destructible, that's going to die, or an immortal soul that is indestructible and cannot be pierced by any weapon cannot be burned by fire. No disease can destroy the soul because the soul is immortal. The soul is all there is. The soul is part of God, and you are that. By developing this practice, we destroy the darkness out of ignorance, our total attachment to our senses, to our body and mind we go beyond. Because we are light, the God in our heart. The same light that shines in heaven in the highest heaven also shines in our heart, and that comes through grace. It's called grace light.

You have to have the company of a saint. You have to have grace in your life. You see the divinity or light in yourself and in others. Then you're able to help others in these chaotic times and burn all your past life karma. It's a great opportunity to serve to share what is obviously the greatest of all your light. It is important that you can serve because Babaji And Jesus say the same thing. In the Bible, John 14 chapter one says, **"Do not let your heart be troubled. You believe in God and also believe in me."** So there you believe in Jesus or Krishna or Allah, or any of their Messiah, teacher or prophet, it doesn't matter. This is time to serve.

One of the greatest gifts to humanity from the Ancient Indian rishis and masters like Babaji is worshiping the fire, which is worshiping the inner light. **Worshiping the fire transforms into pure love, All that is**

impure in heart and mind. The power of the Holy Fire, the flame of love unfolds, the quality of the Soul.

After I met Babaji in 1982, in India, I came back to the U.S. in the Bay area, and started doing the fire ceremony with the devotees who had been to see Babaji and with my friends and family. We created a great community with a lot of love and great energy. People used to come to rejoice and participate in the ceremony. We all sat around a fire and chanted sacred mantras. When I was with Babaji in 1983, he said, do you understand what we are doing? People will think that you're just throwing food in the fire, just burning it. He said it's not just throwing food in the fire. It is a sacrifice you invoke the gods who are in heaven, And when you call on them, they come down, and they receive this offering and in turn, and they bless you and give you a boon.

The purification needs to take place before you become like a child and enter the Gates of Heaven. That's what the Bible says in Matthew, **"Truly, I tell you, unless you change and become like children you will never enter the kingdom of heaven."** Babaji also said, "The fire, the flame of love, unfolds, the quality of the Soul, the worshiping, the fire transforms into pure love and all that is impure in heart and mind."

The first thing I do in the morning as part of the worship is after I take a shower and before breakfast, light a lamp, and if you have a temple altar set up, you light the lamp there. You can light a candle, just like in the church, people light candles all the time–that light is called Jyoti in Sanskrit. You offer the light to a picture of the Guru and all the deities and statues to energize them. You can give them a bath and put Chandan Kumkum. That's the light that shines in our hearts. By offering the light, you are lighting the lamp in your heart too.

Through this process, you develop faith and a relationship with God. Through love, you feel the presence in this daily devotional practice. In this turmoil, what is needed is the good old practice of love and simplicity and not hatred and jealousy. There's a prayer that is sung every morning in the Arti. Arti is offering the lamp, one that removes the suffering, removes the pain. Basically, offering light to a picture or statue removes darkness, which is in our mind and body and the soul, and you become light. Basically, you are filled with light. These are the practices that are required.

Maharishi Mahesh Yogi, who started the TM transcendental meditation movement in the sixties, was a guru of the Beatles said since the Kali yuga started, there is a loss of Gyan Shakti, Gyan Shakti means the power of knowledge that's what's missing right now the knowledge of the soul. People have knowledge of the computer and the internet of artificial intelligence, but they lack real knowledge, the knowledge of their own self and others, and of eternal life. The current youth in India as well the west in the current times have forgotten all the mantras, and there are no qualified teachers to teach how the mantra is correctly pronounced. The correct pronunciation of mantras is very important. Incorrect pronunciation of the mantras can cause more damage to the person for whom the ceremonies are being performed.

There is a Gayatri mantra that was given to humanity by the sage Vishwamitra–the name means a friend of the universe. Thousands of years ago, there was a King Vishwamitra. He went to visit his friend Vashista with his whole force of hundreds of people that traveled with him. Vashista, who was a sage, a monk, living in a remote place. He was welcomed by Vashista, and Vashista said, please have a seat. I will prepare a meal for you and your people.

Vishwamitra said, "How can you in this ashram provide meals for so many people." Vashista had a wish-fulfilling cow, and he asked the cow to give them the food of their choice not only to the King but to all his force that was traveling with him, his guards, his soldiers, his ministers, his Royal servants. All were just fed delicious food of their choice to their satisfaction. The king was totally surprised by this incredible miracle and the power Vashista had. Vishwamitra left his kingdom, And he went to the forest to meditate, to find that power, get that power himself so that he could do miracles. One of the mantras he heard through and is chanted by millions of people all over the world is called Gayatri Mantra. There's actually Gayatri Pariwar of the Gayatri family, who has millions of followers. Gayatri means. one that is sung three times. The first part is "Om Bhur Bhuva Swaha." The second part is "Tat savitur varenyam," and the third part is "Dhiyo yo nah prachodayat."

The sound of the Gayatri mantra gives you the knowledge, gives you the intelligence, which is lost in the KaliYuga. By singing this mantra just ten times destroys the karma or sin committed in one lifetime. Chanting 108 times destroys karma from the past ten lifetimes. So some people chant it like thousand times in the morning and thousand times in the evening. It destroys your karma. Karma is basically the confusion, the darkness, anxiety, or whatever is blocking the flow of light and intelligence because of past actions.

The Gayatri mantra is very, very powerful, and it is a prayer to the sun. The meaning of Gayatri mantra is, "I pray to that light, which has enlightened the entire universe, the lights in heaven to guide my mind and intellect in the right direction." There are so many mantras on the internet, on YouTube, and with the meaning, but the important thing is to recite the mantra and stick with it till you have perfected it.

In my family, this was a mantra, my parents, grandparents used to recite every day, so I just grew up with it. When I went to meet Babaji, an amazing thing happened because he gave me so much attention. People will come from the U.S. or different countries, and he'll talk to them for like 30 seconds, everything, Okay? Then he would just spend, like half an hour talking to me about where are you from, what are you doing? And who do you know, just like when you meet a friend. There was Shastri Ji, his older priest, and there was another older gentleman, his name was Fakirananda, who was living with Babaji in Herakhan ashram at the time. He said, "Your family has done a lot of Gayatri in the past. That's why Babaji is giving you so much attention." Because most people cannot stand next to him for more than like 30 seconds, and some people, he would turn them away and ask them to go back to their country, so you are so fortunate. It is because your ancestors have done so much Gayatri mantra.

Maharishi Mahesh Yogi, brought transcendental meditation to the Beatles and changed the mass consciousness in the sixties and seventies. He said in Kaliyuga what we have lost is the intelligence, the Gyan Shakti, the power of intelligence. Intelligent people don't have hatred, anger, jealousy, pride, and they're full of love, compassion, joy, bliss, harmony and abundance. These are the gifts of the divine, and they can easily be obtained depending on your past karma—by simply repeating the mantra just sounds, secret sounds. You don't have to know the meaning, but if you repeat The Gayatri mantra and visualize the Divine Mother gayatri sitting on a Lotus, and she has five heads. Five heads are our frontal lobe, back of the brain, left brain, the left hemisphere, right hemisphere, and midbrain. The five parts of your brain get activated.

You're able to use the full power of your brain. The Gayatri mantra is for brilliance.

I cannot say enough about it. That's the part of the daily practice. You can destroy the darkness born of ignorance, and by that understanding. You can find God-dwelling in the heart. Babaji said, "I am everywhere. God is closer to you than you think he is actually inside of you." Because you don't have this knowledge, first we don't seek him or those people who seek him. They seek him outside in temples, churches, or mosques. Without the power or knowledge of Gyan Shakti, you cannot find the God Shiva residing in your heart.

The goddess gives you the knowledge and the power so that you know yourself, that you are Shiva, You are God. For that, you need intelligence and brilliance. That comes from the sound, the sound frequency, that activates different parts of your brain. That's the subject of another chapter devoted towards the end, how to activate different parts of the brain, but I just wanted to give you the guide through mantra introduction.

Just one mantra alone, if you chant in the morning, it is best to chant before sunrise, before the sun comes up or while the sun is rising. Also, the sunset because that light will enter your brain, different parts of your brain and literally activate, different parts resulting in the full activation or global activation, with just sound. The mystery of sound is that's what the mantras are, but the current youth have lost interest in the tradition. Because of the time we are living in, people are more worried about making a living and being able to survive. It is time to wake up and develop knowledge of the soul.

There's a pretty sure path, like Krishna says. "Once you come into the company of a saint, someone who has the peace and the knowledge, he can give it to you because you cannot get it Otherwise." I'm giving you this knowledge that I acquired through the company of the saints like Babaji, Muniraj Ji, and numerous other living masters. Right now, the practice of the mantra. Not only the Gayatri mantra, but there are also hundreds and thousands of mantras you can use for living in this current time. Where the massive shift in human consciousness is needed because there will be more earth changes.

Babaji says there are going to be earthquakes, floods, wildfires, natural calamities because there's a need for a shift and a huge shift in collective consciousness because we are so attached to the gross reality that we don't see the light. We don't see the soul. We don't see God. There is a prayer in Sanskrit, "Asato ma jyotirgamaya." That means to take me from darkness to the light and "Mrityorma Amritam gamaya" take me from death to immortality. When you chant the mantra or sound repeatedly, see what happens, there is a nectar that discharges from the brain, and you can feel it in your palate. That is the nectar of immortality called Amrita. There are people with the name Amrita Anand Mayi, which means her name is full of nectar and bliss. The name means she is just immersed in bliss.

The joy or the bliss that comes from the soul comes from the nectar that is inside of you. So, you have to go inside and feel the nectar, drink the nectar. We'll talk about this more in one of the chapters dedicated to the gods. I don't want you to forget the monkey God Hanuman, his favorite God, or Ishta deva is Rama. Hanuman just repeated the name Ram, Ram, Ram, Ram, and he's been doing that for over a hundred thousand years.

When you repeat the same name or the sound, you start tasting this nectar or actually a chemical, if you want to call it that, there's a real transformation that happens within your physical body, this chemical is called DMT (Dimethyltryptamine), so this is what nectar is made of.

You can get drunk with that sound and with that Amrita and experience Amritananda, which is also the name of the mother from Kerala who visits the U.S. every year. I met her when I was young. I used to see her every time would come and visit. She gives you hugs and unconditional love. That is what is needed at this time is unconditional love. You have to open your heart and get filled with the love inside so that you can give it away. There's no lack of anything because we are full. "Purna" means complete and undepleted. You have to connect to the source, Babaji or mother, which is inside of you. By connecting to the source, you become complete.

What that means is once you take something from the whole, it remains whole and is never depleted. You take something from infinity. It still remains infinite. We all are fully complete and undepleted, we have an undepleted source of energy and undepleted abundance, joy, but you have to go within to find it and let go of your identity or your definition of the limited self, which is your ego.

That's what's needed in this time of transition is to get filled with love and with light, with the energy of the source. These mantras can do that. Once you find a teacher like I am being inspired and guided by the divine, so they're speaking through me to give you these words, there are sounds you can use to have an abundance of resources because the sound waves are the building blocks of the entire universe. All galaxies are full of the sound like Shreem called seed mantras. There are a number of long prayers like Durga Saptshati, which can be reduced to a few seed mantras for each chapter. Avadhoot Shiv Baba reduced the seven hundred verses to a few seed sounds for each chapter that you can recite every day.

Herakhan is the name of the place where Babaji appeared in a cave in 1970 And then he meditated on the light in his heart in a cave and called her Haidakhandeshwari or Haidakhan Eshwari, the goddess of Haidakhan. Vishnu Datt Shashtri Ji, who was his head priest, wrote 700 verses in praise of that Divine Mother and called it Haidakhnadi Saptashati. One of the verses in Sanskrit is, "Haida Khandeshwari Payat Sarvalok Maheshwari Dayamurti dhara nityam Vishwa santean tatpara." She is the mother and goddess of the entire galaxy, all Lokas, and she is forever engaged in the welfare of the entire universe. She is the light that shines in our hearts. Babaji, manifested and materialized a body in the cave of Herakhan in 1970.

Still today, you can feel the presence of the goddess, where nine beautiful temples have been built by Babaji. Babaji is always sitting in a cave somewhere in the Himalayas, meditating on that light and continuously engaged in the welfare of the entire universe. Whoever says Babaji receives the instant blessing, just like what Yogananda said in his book. If you meditate on the mother in the cave of your heart, you receive her blessing, you destroy all your ignorance, all your misfortune in an instant just by remembering her.

This is just one of the prayers from the 700 verses that Shashtri Ji created. I recite all 700 of them in the morning, every day because when I met Shashtri Ji in Herakhan, he had just written and published these 700 verses in praise of Haidakhandeshwari. Shashtri Ji was giving out this book. I got one of the first few copies from him, and he said, if you read every day and do havan with this, you will become a siddha, and I got Babaji to bless it on top of that. I took it to Babaji during darshan, and he just touched it. Then I went to the Hiadakhandeshwari's temple on the cave side just above the cave. I sat in front of the mother and recited the whole Haidakhandi saptashati for her. Babaji came by during his morning darshan of the nine temples he built and blessed me again in front of the temple.

Then I memorized it. It is sitting on my tongue. I memorized all 700 verses step-by-step, but Shashtri Ji said, if you do a fire ceremony with this, you'll become a Siddha accomplished master, master with supernormal powers. I just started reading it in the morning after I finished Arti or offering the lamp to the Deity. Then I sat down and read the Saptashati that Shashtri Ji told me to do. I also did parts of the Durga saptashati reading as directed by Shri Muniraj Ji. There was an opportunity in 2010 to perform a huge fire ceremony in Florida at the time of Makar Sankranti when there are no evil spirits on the planet.

The Sun visits Saturn and in Hindu mythology. Saturn is a son of the Sun, but they are enemies because Saturn is born out of Chaya, which is the shadow of the sun. Saturn was not happy with his father, Sun, so on the Makar sankranti, they visited each other. There's no evil spirit on the planet, so we did a huge fire ceremony in Fort Lauderdale with the Babaji Devotees. After the ceremony, we went to the ocean. We went to the beach to take a bath because that's the tradition in India. On that day, people go to a sacred river for purification and to start a new life.

We did that, and after the bath, we saw there was a huge sound and light pillar right in front of us above the sea. The Divine Mother appeared from heaven, and the space between heaven and the earth was filled with light and loud noises as if there's heavy rain coming down to earth. It was filled with light and sound. All the girls that were on the beach just started screaming with joy. They came and surrounded me from all sides in ecstasy. This was an incredible blessing and demonstration of the power of sound. The power of the sound and the divine is incredible. Repeat the mantra and she will appear in front of you if your heart is pure. If you're dedicated, and if you've surrendered and you have a teacher who is a siddha or siddheshwar then you can also become an enlightened master.

So that's where I got my first experience. Even before that, the mother had appeared to me. We will talk about the experience more during the goddess chapter. But since we're talking about living in the present, in current times you need the Shakti, the knowledge, and like Maharishi Mahesh Yogi has said that Gyan Shakti has disappeared from the planet. That's why the dark age Kaliyuga is here, but she's very available. You just have to know the technique, how to approach her, how to invoke her, because she's inside your heart. At the same time, she's everywhere. Hreem is the one sound of the Holy Spirit that pervades the entire universe.

I was there in one of the Babaji Ashrams in a remote Kumaon village called Chlianaula. Muniraj Ji created an ashram for Babaji, and there was a nine-day celebration going on. I was telling Muniraj Ji, How hard it is to live in the West because of all this work-related stress and so many problems living in the world. During Navrati's nine days, there are three days dedicated to Kali and the three days are dedicated to Lakshmi, and three days are dedicated to Saraswati. During the first few days during the power time of Kali, I was talking to Muniraj Ji. I said I need

Kali's blessing. I got a small idol of Kali from one of the ashram stores and got Muniraj Ji to bless it.

After Navratri, I was taking a massage and in the Ayurvedic Hospital next to the ashram in India. They give you a herbal oil massage. You take a steam bath after the massage. I was sitting in this steam bath, and all this oil that they massage you with was oozing out of me from every pore of my skin, just sweating profusely. That's when I had a vision of Kali, she appeared to me with our two red eyes and the third eye, with her red tongue, and she was holding a chopped head with blood pouring from her hand. I was not praying to do anything. I was just relaxing after the massage. The mother appears to me with four arms, and the joy of seeing her, just feeling, is unbelievable. I was not afraid of the blood or the chopped head. The Goddess is there, will give you the knowledge, she will give you power, but you have to surrender to them. You have to dedicate your life first. You have to believe that they're real and they're closer to you than you think. They will come, they're already in your heart, but you can make them alive. You can have them appear in front of you. So, after that day, my life just changed completely. When I came back to the U.S., I was telling my brother-in-law about this experience. He was asking, how was your trip? And I was telling him about what happened? He said, "Oh, if you chant the Kali mantra and she'll appear, God is there." There are thousands of goddesses everywhere in every city. There like more than 5,000 temples in Varanasi. That's what you do–have faith, surrender and keep the company of saints and she will appear when you call on her in time of need.

CHAPTER 5

Lessons from Ramayana & Mahabharata

Ramayana provides deep insights not only into human nature, but the means to utilize the human mind for maximum fulfillment in life - both on the individual level as well as on the collective level.

The antagonist in the Ramayana Ravana is considered to be one of the most learned, skilled, as well as valiantly gifted in history -

Having acquired great power, wealth and wisdom, he is invincible. Yet, it was one weakness that brought about his inevitable downfall.

That one weakness has plagued many individuals and many otherwise accomplished leaders - that of an unbridled ego that often gets hopelessly out of hand.

When one forgets the very source of one's strength and success, the mistaken intellect begins to assume its own greatness devoid of its connection to its source."

~ Maharishi Mahesh Yogi

This is a time of great collective purification of consciousness because of the transition from the dark age to the golden age. Every time that happens, there's great turmoil and great changes in the humanities mindset and heart set because the thought process is needed to shift from lower to higher consciousness. During this transition, all the suffering is caused by Maya and the ego, which is our greatest enemy. We have three choices to deal with our past karma–either we don't do anything and suffer, or serve others, or meditate. There's a great opportunity to serve others and discover our true selves.

When I was growing up in Varanasi, there was an analogy very commonly used to compare living in the world with crossing an ocean called Bhava Sagara. Bhava is the world, and Sagar is the ocean. The world is like an ocean you have to cross, from birth to death, or sometimes they call it Bhava Coupa, or worldly deep well, which is like a pothole. Sometimes kids playing fall into a deep well, and they have to be rescued. We're so engrossed in our worldly affair that we fall into a pothole very deep, and then someone has to use ropes or chains to pull you out of the pothole. So liberation is like pulling you out of this pothole or realm of suffering,

People are going through the suffering, and divine help is available when you ask. When you call unto Babaji, Jesus or divine in any form, any name Krishna Allah, any Messiah or prophet you know then the help comes, and you're liberated from the suffering. As soon as you know who you are, there is no more suffering because you realize that you're God. For God, there is no limitation. Nothing is impossible. I'm sure the reason we get in big trouble is because there are some do's and don't. We don't observe or are not aware of the Dharma of living in the world. The liberation is achieved when you follow Dharma and burn all your past life karma because we are all one eternal soul that has no beginning and no end.

We have been playing this game of life on the planet earth as long as Mother Earth has been around, which is estimated to be like 3-4 billion years. That's how old we are. We have been living in different forms for billions of years. We have had millions of lives, multiple innumerable countless lives or complex lives. In those lives, what happens is that we accumulate karma, our thought process, and that's what's called Karma, our mindset, body set, soul set. We've talked about earlier when I was growing up in India, all these scriptures, including Vedas, the book of ancient wisdom, describe the natural law of helping others and these are described as righteousness in the Bible or kindness, loving-kindness, or serving others.

Our goal is to find liberation or freedom, freedom from all suffering and, and enjoy the bliss that is our true nature of the self. All the negative mental projections that we have, if you don't like somebody, hatred, jealousy are a result of past life karma. The past life karma keeps blocking out positive energy from being absorbed. The past karma must be removed through meditation, glorification, worship, and spiritual purification.

There are many practices I learned when I was growing up. I was surrounded by my parents and grandparents. Most of my ancestors were always singing praise to Hanuman from Ramayana, who is one of the seven immortals who live forever. You probably saw a picture of the monkey god. Who is always repeating the name of his Ishta Dev or favorite God Rama? Just by remembering Rama, Rama not only stays very alert, but he can also accomplish an impossible task easily. Rama is the King of all the galaxies, but he appeared as a human being, and Hanuman took birth to serve him, fell in love with him, and became his servant. Rama made his journey on our earth plane as an avatar who lived an ideal life of a husband, son, brother, and king. He came down from heaven and ruled for 10,000 years with his wife Sita.

There is a scripture called *Ramayana* that is read every day by millions of people in India. Just by remembering Lord Ram's or his past times or what he did in eleven thousand years on the earth plane, just by pondering on it or just listening to him, you will not fall into this Kupa or pothole of worldly suffering. That means just by singing the glory, praising the Lord, you are liberated. *Ramayana* was written about 500 years ago by Goswami Tulsidas.

There was a lot of conflict between Hindus and Muslims at that time when Ramayana was written. Just by remembering or listening to the stories of Rama, you don't get lost in the world. That means you don't get drowned in the ocean of the world, get old and die. You don't get overwhelmed with the challenges and suffering of the world. What is suggested is to learn from what happened when there were challenges, and an avatar descends from heaven, in the times of Rama and Krishna, the two avatars.

We are going to talk about Mahabharata, which is the Great War that took place when Krishna was living on the earth plane. Every time the dharma declines, the people start suffering and the people start crying. God himself appears, so it says in the Bhagavad Gita every time the dharma declines, Krishna says I myself create a body and come down to restore the Dharma on the earth.

Rama also did the same thing. Saint-poet Tulsidas says the same thing in his language:

"Jab jab hoi dharm ke hani,
Barhi asur Adham abhimani,
Tab Prabhu Dhari vividh sharira
Harhi Kripanidhi Sajjan pira"

That means every time the dharma declines and the demons and the wicked people become powerful, strong, and they start torturing noble people, then God takes different forms to remove the pain and suffering of the noble people in the world.

That's why Rama was born. This is why listening to the life story of Rama gives you so much courage, and strength increases your faith, and gives you the power to live in the Kaliyuga, in the dark ages, and face life as it comes to you. Rama was faced many challenges and lived like a normal person, and his own wife was kidnapped. Not only that, he was going to be sworn as a King, his stepmother said, "No, I want my son to be the king. He had to go to the forest for 14 years with his newlywed wife," and he said, "Oh, that's great. I can enjoy the company of the saints, the learned men who live in the forest and meditate," and he gladly accepted this. Not only that, his wife was kidnapped by this demon King Ravana, who had lived in Lanka, or now it's called Sri Lanka. Ravana owned the whole island of Sri Lanka, and he had a whole island built of gold, with hundreds and thousands of maids and servants.

But he still wanted Rama's wife, Sita. Somebody had told him that Rama's wife is the most beautiful woman on the planet, so he kidnapped her, and Rama had to go and find his wife. He had no help. He was just with his brother–Lakshman. Then he met Hanuman, the Monkey God. The whole story is documented in Ramayana. There's an English translation available, but Rama does not lose his courage, does not lose his faith, does not lose his cool during these challenging times. He had a firm belief that he could find his wife. He can find who kidnapped his wife. He was able to travel on foot in India from North, where Ayodhya is currently located, to the southern tip of India, Rameshwaram, which is several thousand miles. They traveled by foot through the different mountains, and they were able to rescue his wife and killed the demon King with the help of Hanuman. That's why it's really uplifting just to listen to the story from *Ramayana*. Coming back to Hanuman. He says, "Kah Hanumant vipati Prabhu soi

Jab tab sumiran bhajan na hoi." Hanuman says the trouble comes only when you really don't even remember and praise the Lord.

And for him, nothing is impossible because he has tremendous faith in Rama. He is able to fly in the air. He is able to lift a mountain. Because during the war, what happened when Rama and Hanuman were fighting this demon, King Ravana, in the southern part of India? His younger brother, whose name is Lakshman, was hurt in a war, and he became unconscious. The doctor or medicine man was called, and he said, there is a herb called Sanjeevani on the mountain called Dronagiri in North Himalaya, if Hanuman can get it, then I can bring your brother Lakshman back to life. Hanuman flew to North to get this Sanjeevani booti or herb. Sanjeevani means life-giving herbs. Hanuman was flying. He went up to that mountain, and he could not figure out which herbs to get. He picked up the whole mountain, and he flew with that mountain down South to where Lakshman was unconscious. He was given a time limit. He had to be returned before the sun came up. He had given a very short time, but Hanuman was able to do that because Hanuman has tremendous powers.

Hanuman represents the power of faith. We'll talk about Hanuman more in the next chapter. I trust it is the faith that carries you through, and Hanuman is a great example. The same thing happened at the time of Krishna, Mahabharata the Great War happened. There was a huge war that took place because there was a big dispute over the inheritance of this royal kingdom between the two cousin families, and the two cousins were the Pandavas and Kauravas. Pandavas are five brothers, and other cousins were called Kauravas, and they were a hundred brothers. Now, what happened Kauravas were like caretakers of this huge kingdom which spread all over India because Pandavas were very young, they could not inherit the kingdom so they had given the power to just a caretaker.

When the five Pandava brothers grew up, they asked for their share. They were refused. The Kauravas said, "No way! You don't get anything!"

Krishna was involved in the negotiation. He went back to the court, and he said, "This is their kingdom. They're your cousins. Will you give them half of the kingdom? If you cannot give half, how about giving them five villages so that they can have their own land and they can feed their family."

The oldest of the Kauravas, his name was Duryodhana, said, "You're talking about five villages. I'm not going to give them even as much land as the tip of a needle."

Krishna, even though he showed his power and the form all-pervading in the entire universe, from the earth to heaven, filled up the whole space and showed them who he was, but even then, Kauravas did not surrender to him. They said, "No, you're not getting any land."

So Krishna said that you leave me no alternative but war. He became a messenger of peace first when there was no other alternative–they had to resort to war. What happened during the war?

They said to Krishna, "You are too powerful. You cannot take part in the war."

Krishna said, "No, I will not lift any weapon. I will be just a driver for Arjuna, and I'll drive his chariot on the horses."

The Kauravas chose the huge force of Krishna, whereas the Pandavas chose to be with Krishna and who promised not to carry any weapon. Kauravas' side had the most powerful warriors, including the guru. His name was Dronacharya. He's the one who actually trained all the warriors on both sides. Their grandfather's name was Bhishma. He was very, very powerful. The war lasted 18 days. The hundred Kaurvas brothers were all killed, including Krishna's huge army.

The message of the Mahabharata is that no matter how powerful, how strong you are, how much money you have, how much army force you have, if you are On the wrong side of the Dharma, then you are going to be a loser. In the end, the truth wins. There is a saying in Sanskrit, which is very popular, and it was popularized by Mahatma Gandhi when I was growing up. He says, "Satyamev Jayate," which means the truth always wins no matter how weak it may seem. As Krishna has mentioned, Dharma is always the winner. This is what's going on right now.

The lesson from the great war is fully documented in great detail in "18,000 verses of Maha Bharat" by Sage Veda Vyasa. The lesson from the war again is the truth, love, and light always wins. That's why we want to be on the side of Dharma, of the righteousness, of the love of helping people, and being kind to those who are less fortunate than we are. The other lesson from the Mahabharata is karma, and it is very hard for people to believe. First of all, they had a past life, and they have some karma, but I wanted to use the stories from Mahabharata as an example, to show you that whatever happens to you has a reason, and there's always past life karma involved. For example, when Kauravas lost a hundred sons and their father DhritaRashtra, who happened to be blind anyway, asked Krishna, "Why me? Why? What have I done wrong to lose a hundred sons?" in the war with their cousins.

Dhristrashtra could meditate, and he could see his past lives. He said, "I've not done anything wrong in the past hundred lives, past hundred births. So Krishna, please tell me why I lost my hundred sons."

Krishna sat down to meditate and told Dhritrashtra that in one hundred and second birth before the current birth. "You were supposed to watch a couple of swans for a Brahmin couple who went on a pilgrimage, but after the Brahmin couple left for the pilgrimage. The Swan couple gave birth to a hundred babies that you consumed, and upon their return, when the Brahman learned about the loss of the hundred swans, he cursed you. You suffered the loss of a hundred sons. For this reason, all your hundred sons were killed."

The next story is of the grandfather who raised the Kauravas and Pandava, whose name was Bhishma Pitamah. The grandfather was killed by his dear grandson Arjuna. He laid on a deathbed, made of arrows. He asked Krishna the same thing. "Krishna, why am I suffering on the death bed of arrows that were made by my grandson, whom I have raised and fed him his favorite food that I've cooked for him and fed him with my own hands? I have not done anything wrong as far as I can see for the past 70 lives."

Then Krishna told him that, look, you've not done anything wrong the past 70 lives, but you have done a similar act in a previous life, 72 lives before the current life. You have killed someone you love by similar death. You have to pay for your karma as you do, so shall you reap."

The moral of this story is that you cannot get liberated till you are free of your past life karma and karmic debts. By serving others and helping others, you pay back some of the karmic debt. That's why all the religions and enlightened beings, including Jesus, say love and serve others like you love and serve me, and Babaji said the same thing. Love others as I have loved you. Serving humanity is serving God. Sai Baba used to say, "Manav Seva is Madhava Seva." That means serving humanity is serving God. The third important lesson from the Great War is surrender. Krishna told Arjun on the battleground of Mahabharata, "Forget all the religions. you just surrender to me totally, and I will free you from all your past sins and give you liberation."

The easiest way to get liberation and get freedom from all your past karma is to totally surrender. Shiva Purana says, "Only by total complete surrender to Shiva can you achieve liberation. Even if you read all the Vedas, numerous times you cannot get liberation."

What's needed? Here's a change of heart. Jesus also says that "I will take out your stony heart and fill you with the Holy Spirit." Babaji is also closely working with Jesus on awakening the human heart. In the beginning, we talked about this–God lives in our hearts. There is a prayer that we sing every day in Herakhan Arati "Antar hridaya shudh shiv vasa, Pahichanahu taji agya durasa." Meaning in the inner chamber of your heart, a pure heart. God resides, one who recognizes that will be free." That's what liberation is recognizing the God in your own self and then in all. For that, total surrender and a change of heart, and purifying all your karma is required. The complete, true surrender to God takes care of your karma.

There are many stories of when I met Babaji when Babaji was living in flesh and blood, in a body between 1970 and 1984 in the village called Herakhan where I went with my mother and two younger brothers at the time and surrendered to him completely. You have to surrender your ego that I am somebody. Basically, you disappear. Only God remains. I talked about this earlier so that there's only one of us. There is no me and you. There are other saints in the past in India that surrendered their ego and became one with God.

There was a very famous Krishna lover. His name was Kripalu Ji Maharaj. He still has a huge following. He has an ashram in Vrindavan, and he is on TV. He has his own channel every day where people are singing and glorifying Krishna. Here is another example of how he surrendered himself to God, so that he became God. Then he had a huge following after that. One of his followers came to my neighbor's house when I was living near Boston. At my neighbor's house, there was satsang and kirtan. I was singing to Radha very joyfully with my neighbors that night Kripalu Ji came to me in a dream even though I never met him. Total transformation is possible only when you surrender, and then the love of God starts flowing through you, not only love of God, but the nectar or Amrita of God will flow through chanting, And so this is the practice. By daily practice, totally surrendering the mind to God or his name or mantra so that only the name remains, the only mantra remains not the mind.

There are others who also by surrender became one with Krishna. Mira Bai was a young girl born in a very royal family in Rajasthan. When she was very young, like five or six years old, she saw a huge Indian wedding ceremony of a couple. She went to her mom, and she asked her mother, mom, mom, where is my bridegroom, who am I going to marry?

Her mother just said jokingly, Krishna is your husband, your bridegroom. You are going to marry Krishna. She, from a very young age, started singing to Krishna. There are many devotional songs of Meera Bai full of so much love for Krishna. A very famous song is "Mere to Giridhar Gopal Dusro na koi." Only Giridhar Gopal is mine, no one else. She fell totally in love with Krishna, even though she had never seen him. She would just go to the people who were older and ask about Krishna. She went to poet Raidas and other saints and asked them about Krishna. Then she would just sing and dance to Krishna all the time, even though she was married. She left her husband for Krishna, and eventually, Krisna appeared to her at midnight at the bank of a river. She merged into him and disappeared. That is the total surrender by Mirabai.

There have been so many movies made on Mirabai. There have been so many books that are written on Mirabai. The songs from Mirabai are very, very famous and very full of love and emotion to Krishna. She used to say, "Mere to Giridhar Gopal." That means that my lover is Gopal, who had lifted a mountain. Krishna had lifted a mountain when he was young on his pinky at the request of the villagers that could not stop a huge rain that was coming down. He had lifted this mountain just to protect his friends and neighbors or villagers by his pinky. His name is Giridhar, there's one other name of Krishna called Gopal, the one who takes care of the cows. Krishna used to wear a peacock feather in his crown. So she says, "The one who has in his crown, a peacock feather, he's my husband." So that is ultimate love, merging into Krishna or your lover.

Those who are interested in it should follow Bhakti yoga or love yoga. Through devotion, through love yoga, you can merge with your lover and become one with him. Babaji, during his last days before entering Mahasamdhi used to listen to Meerabi songs on his Herakhan kutir balcony in the early morning while giving darshan. I spent a lot of time with him during Christmas of 1983 with my family, enjoying the Mirabai songs, which have become an unforgettable memory for the whole family.

Through Bhakti or love yoga, you can merge into God, who lives everywhere and who also lives in your heart. This is a path called Bhakti yoga, and now it's called love yoga. By loving the divine, you can totally, completely merge into him and become free, become limitless, and become light who you really are.

CHAPTER 6

We are light

"The inner light itself is regarded as self-knowledge by the holy ones and the experience of it is an integral part of self-knowledge and non-different from it. He who has self-knowledge is forever immersed in the experience of it. He is liberated while living and lives like an emperor of the world."
~ Vasishta's Yoga

"God is light and in him is no darkness at all."
~ John 1.5

There is a light that shines beyond all things on earth beyond us all beyond the heavens beyond the highest the very highest heavens. This is the light that shines in our heart." ~ Chandogya Upanishad 3.13.7

"Who should know him with heart and mind becomes immortal."
~ Shvetashvatara Upanishad

So everything you see as the visual matter is made of light or photons or divine light. There is a light that shines in our hearts, and you can see it in meditation. Swami Muktananda, the founder of Siddha yoga, who lived in the seventies and eighties, wrote a book called *Chit Shakti Vilas*, or "Play of Consciousness." In that he describes how he was able to see the blue pearl in meditation. He used to get up at four in the morning when it was really quiet, and then he would just meditate. Then he saw this blue light blue pearl, the light that shines in our hearts. And Babaji talks about that light as the Divine Mother Haidakhandeshwari. Mahendra Maharaj called her Jyothirmayi jagdishi, the brilliant shining light of the mother of Haidakhan. There are 700 verses written by Vishnu Dutt Shastri Ji for the mother that lives in his heart. All forms are her form. "Amba amba jai jagdamba. Sarva Rupa ek tuhi amba."

Because Babaji lived in a cave and meditated on the divine mother in the cave of his heart for a very, very long time, he could give her a form of a forever young consort of Haidakhan Babaji. It takes a long time to see the mother in your heart. The light is there. It takes a long time to see the light in your heart. It is the Holy Spirit. Jesus said, I'm gonna leave a comforter behind, that will do all the miracles. Babaji said I would leave the mother behind. So light is the mother, and that creates everything. That light is inside of us.

She is a mother who permeates the entire universe in the form of sound. The mother also has a vibration or sound counterpart, which is the seed mantra-like Hreem, Shreem, Kleem. These are all the sound frequency or vibration of the light, which is in our hearts. We are made of that light. By praying to the light, you can get all your desires fulfilled because she is all in all. There are various intimate ways of approaching the mother because she's inside our heart and mind because your soul is made of light. In one of the Upanishad, there is a prayer, it says, "Lord of light, the knowing one, the golden guardian, the giver of life to all. Spread apart thy rays gather up thy brilliance so that I may perceive thy most splendorous nature that cosmic spirit Which is in my heart for I myself am that."

What is the cosmic spirit or Holy Spirit? That is the light, and it shines in your heart. Now why we don't see it is because we don't spend time on it. We have been fortunate to have a guru who's been there, done that, and show us the way. Swami Muktananda talked about how he saw the blue light within "The Play of Consciousness." I was living in San Diego back in '89. And that's when I first got hold of that book. My kids were young, I was working, but when I found that book and I started reading it one night, I could not put it down. I went to another room, and I started reading it. I must have read, like half of that book called "The Play of Consciousness." I could not stop reading for hours. Then I fell asleep as he was talking about how everything is a play of consciousness and how he left his mother, that he loved so much.

During that night, Baba Muktananda appeared to me in a dream, and that's an incredible experience. I have never met Swami Sri Muktananda. In that dream, I was traveling with him, and I was sitting on his chair. He had all his followers come and worship me and wash my feet. I was totally transformed by this darshan and initiation and Shakti pat. I told my wife what happened. So I used to go to the Siddha Yoga Meditation center in San Diego near where I work in Sorrento Valley. I used to go at night, I think once a week, they did chanting and Aarti. It was one of the favorite Chants there, "Jyot Se Jyot jagao sadguru Jyot se Jyot jagao. Sadguru Jyot se Jyot jagao." By lighting one flame from another Sadguru, remove the darkness.

What that means is light my fire or Jyot, which is inner light or flame. So light my inner flame and remove all the darkness–that was the prayer they sang every night. Light up my lamp with your lamp, just like you light a candle with another candle. So, light up my own heart and remove my inner darkness. That's what the group does. Only a sadguru can remove the inner darkness, and then we become aware of that light because we don't ever go deep and think that we are light and made of light.

In Haidakhan ashram, there is a similar prayer. "Hey mother, you are the mother of the universe. You are in every form. You take every form you are in everyone. Only you alone are everything. Every form is your form." That is the power of the mother, and there are people who spend their life just worshiping the mother and light because she truly is the essence of everything. Jesus always talks about the light. You cannot see the light within your heart unless your mind is enlightened. That's why we've prayed to the sun or the light of the sun through the Gayatri mantra. I pray to the light that illuminates the entire cosmos. Please light up my mind and guide me in the right direction, So that we can see the light within. That is the power of the light, even Paramahansa Yogananda who founded the SRF, very close to where I live in Encinitas, there is a huge hermitage on the seashore that talks about the light of the Divine Mother. SRF was founded by Babaji himself and then handed down to Sri Yukteshwsr Giri by Lahiri Mahasaya.

The whole essence of Kriya yoga is to see the light within, and it takes a lot of discipline, a lot of breathing practices, and the control of mind, and then you eventually meditate on the light within, and different colors in your heart and it gives you incredible bliss and self-realization, so that's what the self-realization fellowship is. All the great religions and the great traditions of the past meditate on the light. I've got to share a very well-known teacher Agastya who gave Aditya Hridya stotra to Rama, the great avatar when he was struggling to fight and defeat the demon king Ravana in Sri Lanka in the Southern part of India.

Rama was contemplating attacking Ravana, who was very powerful And at the time had a huge force, and Rama, as an avatar, was alone just with his brother and the monkeys of Hanuman. Agastya muni gave him this mantra to pray to the sun, Aditya Hridaya Stotram, which is in your heart. The sun is the one who makes up everything. He can give you the victory in your fight with the demon. Ramah recited that Adiutya Hridaya stotra three times, and he was able to get victory over Ravana, who was undefeated, unconquerable, until that time. That is the power of the light. With light or power, you can conquer all enemies, fulfill all desires and, and become one with everything in the universe. Because she is the mother of all, all the goddesses, all the women are goddesses and are basically made of light. That's why we say Amba, Amba. Mother is everything. Light is everything. Everything is light and the more you meditate on it, It will remove the darkness born out of ignorance. You can do a simple meditation. You can meditate on one of the mantras.

If you don't know Sanskrit, then you can just meditate on the light going into your two eyes, and then the third eye and imagine a very bright light entering your ears, entering your mouth, entering your nostrils, and entering your throat through your mouth and filling your heart chakra, entering your brain and filling the entire body from the top of the head to the tailbone, your feet, knees, every part. Basically, you become the light itself. Your body no longer exists. The remainder is the light. By meditating on the name of the Lord of the Light, you become the light. The body disappears. There is only the light, and that's what you are. That's how you achieve victory over death. You just merge into the light, so that is the power of the light. This is what you are, and there will be more meditation as we go towards the end.

There are several meditations on the light. You can visualize light as different colors of the rainbow entering from the top of your head from violet, indigo, blue, green, yellow, orange, red, seven colors coming down and filling your seven chakras, starting from the top of the head crown, and the third eye in the middle of the eyebrows and the throat chakra, and then the heart chakra, and then navel chakra and the second chakra and the root chakra. Those are the seats of the light, and different seed mantras and different sounds. When we talk about chakras later, we can get more familiar with it to purify your being and purify all your karma. As you purify your karma, all your past programming that is stored in your different chakras is removed. You're able to achieve a lightness of being and become a new person. We will end this chapter, and we'll come back to the light and Chakras and meditation in the subsequent chapters.

CHAPTER 7

DEVOTION - love yoga

"Who should know him with heart and mind becomes immortal."

~ Svetasvatara Upanishad IV:20

Devotion to God and the nine forms of devotion. Why do we need to develop devotion to God? Because by living in the world and doing our daily duties, we forget who we are, and we have lost our connection to God, who resides in our own hearts. At the same time, he's also controlling the whole universe, just like an instrument. That's what he is saying in the Gita through his Maya, through his illusion. He runs the entire world, but he is at the same time closer to you than you think. He knows your every thought, and he is inside of you. But we never feel that connection. We feel so far away from God and his omniscience. God knows everything, and God is omnipotent. He can do everything. God is omnipresent. God is everywhere, but still, we feel lost in the world.

Devotion is the easiest way to get closer to God and get to know God thru love or love yoga. Love yoga is basically loving guru or the god. What happens is that the devotion is basically purifying our intellect. Our intellect needs to be purified because we have anger, hatred, jealousy, anxiety, fear, which need to be removed from the intellect.

Devotion is the way to do it. God has given us a process to connect with your own self. God lives in us as our joy, our bliss, our unlimited intelligence. They call it infinite intelligence and the infinite consciousness and bliss, which is all inside. But how do we connect with him? So we have the whole body. Our body is made up of five elements. Then, we have five senses, and the five elements are earth, water, fire, air, and space. The five senses are our senses of touch, senses of smell, senses of hearing, seeing, and taste. Basically, our eyes, our ears, our nostrils, our tongue, and our skin. These five elements make up who we are, and then the five senses mostly turn outwards or delude us by the different appearance and experience of the Maya, which is God appearing in different forms.

Even though he is one, he appears to us as many. Devotion or love yoga removes the veil between you and Him. If you love somebody, then you want to know everything about him. When you love God, the first thing in devotion is you have to love yourself because you're God. God is closest to you than anything. He is inside of you as you, and that is your real identity. You are not your body, how old you are, where you were born, Who's your mother and father. That's not your real self. You are God. Aham Brahmasmi, everybody's made in the image of God. By doing any of the nine forms of devotion, you can realize your oneness with God.

There are nine forms of devotion that are given in the scriptures, like the one I'm going to talk about first. The first process is Shravanam or just listening when you listen to the story of God from someone like I gave you an example of Mirabai because Meera when she was very young, and her mother told her that your husband is Krishna. She was like five, six years old and she started playing with him and his statue and wanted to get to know him, find out more about him and started singing to him.

Listening to stories and different names of God is using your sense of hearing. Your sense of hearing is connected to space. The space is full of this sound–Nada, or the word of god. In the beginning, was the God with whom was the word, so first thing, you're listening to the word of sound. You sit in silence and listen, or you listen to devotional songs or Kirtan. The first thing to engage in any devotional practice or activity is listening.

The second one is Kirtanam or singing like praise of the Lord in Christianity–it's the same thing. Some people sing hallelujah in India. There are so many people who just sing loudly all the time, like people who follow Krishna. They sing his name or stories in poems from saint-poets of India. The people who follow Shiva sing his name and talk about the mythological stories–singing is the next way.

This is how we engage all our senses that are normally extroverted. We were trying to go in. We're trying to find and connect with the God who is living in the heart. So singing is one way, you sing to him. Most people will get up and sing to Krishna in a group. Like Mirabai used to get up and sing to Krishna, and we talked about her famous song "Mere to Giridhar Gopal" that I only have Gopala Krishna and nobody else. So you have to develop your own way, your favorite tune or melody that connects you to joy, it's very joyful, it's very blissful to sing, or just listen to somebody who is full of love and devotion. There are millions of songs available, and based on your past life, you may connect with a certain avatar like Jesus, or there are so many goddesses songs that are very moving.

The next thing you can do to connect with God is by simply remembering or reflecting on meeting with Guru as God. If you have a memory of the past just like you think about your grandmother or grandfather or memory of when you were young and used to have a happy life, and when you were happy. I think of the time in Banaras, even when I was growing up and I used to go to the golden Shiva temple of Kashi Vishwanath right in front of my house, which was surrounded by templates everywhere. I used to think of it every morning, and I have some pictures of the other temple and deities. I look at it and instantly get in touch with those beings, just like imaginary friends who are gods, actually. You're getting in touch with a God who is inside of you.

Remembering is the third way—one of the religions in India is Sikh. A religion whose teacher was Guru Nanak, and they emphasize constant remembrance of the Guru and his words or sumiran very heavily. It is just a reflection. It is not just memory–it is like thinking about God, thinking about someone you love. I still think about my grandmother, who used to spend so much time just singing in devotion to God, and her whole life was dedicated to devotion only. Remembering God is the easiest way to connect with God that is called Sumiran followed by serving the Lord and making him more real in your life. For most people, God does not exist. This is for the ones who believe, one way to get closer to God by serving him. How do you serve him? You can serve him as you're serving your close family, family members, your neighbors, your colleagues, and the others who are less fortunate than you. Traditionally in India, people build a small temple in their home where they actually have deities. I have a small temple. We have all the deities and the statues that my grandmother used to have and used to bathe them first thing in the morning after you take a shower.

Before you have breakfast, you put on clean clothes, then you go, and you do your Seva. Seva means you're serving them just like you have the kids like you have little babies, so you wake them up, you give them a bath, you put on new clothes for them, then you feed them. Before we feed them, you offer some lights using candles or ghee lamps. There is a very simple but very powerful ceremony called Aarati, or offering of lights. You pray and sing Aarti in all the temples of India. Serving, waking up God is very elaborately celebrated with a lot of ingredients. There are 16 different activities called Shodashopachara. What you're trying to do is offer the five elements and that make up your five senses and get more insight into your true self. Through this ceremony the true self Shiva enters your body, mind and soul. It gets you more connected with God. We will talk more about that.

Bathing in itself is called abhishekam, with the five elements we call Panchamrit. Basically, it's sugar, yogurt, milk, honey, and clarified butter. You offer those five ingredients to the deity, whether it's Krishna or Shiva, it could be a statue of Jesus or Mother Mary, whoever is your Ishta Deva or your favorite deity. You offer to them, and you bathe them, and you purify them. Then you do the worshiping or Archana. In worshiping, again, there are so many processes and mantras practiced for centuries that have been documented for Shiva called Rudrabhishekam.

You basically ask for what you want, but you praise the Lord first. Then Archana is done in most of the temples. If you go to an Indian temple, they will do an Archana for you. They will chant 108 names of the deity and offer 108 times flowers on your behalf and ask your wishes to be granted. Worshiping the Lord takes different forms. For example, the Neem Karoli Baba is a very well-known saint in India. People like Steve Jobs and even Mark Zuckerberg went to see him. Mark Zuckerberg recently, when he met the Indian prime minister, talked about his visit when he was having problems with starting his Facebook business. He was recommended by Steve Jobs, who had met him earlier.

The Neem Karoli Baba ashram in Germany does Hanuman chalisa every morning and evening. They sing 40 complex couplets in praise of Hanuman. It just purifies your intellect, and you have no other thought in your mind than just praising the Lord. Worshiping basically is like requesting them something, but God already knows what you want. Worshiping is a very much part of Christianity also. There's worship most people are familiar with the midnight mass at St. Peter's Basilica in Rome. There is a standard procedure for every Ashram worldwide for Babaji. I adopted my own practice based on that. There is a bathing or hydration ceremony first thing in the morning while singing and worshiping, you offer a lot of fruit, a lot of sweets.

We will talk more about this when we get into rituals and meditation chapters, but worshiping the Lord is just dedicating your mind and your body and soul to God, focusing on the Lord you merge with God. Then there are millions of prayers. You have to find the one that is closest to your heart. You have to find the one deity that you connect with, again, based on your past life history. We have lived millions of lives, and you probably had a life or several lives in India, in Banaras as Banaras is the oldest, continuous living city older than Rome and Jerusalem. Most people have lived there, and they connect to a certain form of worship, a certain form of Deity.

As you start embarking on this path, you will connect with certain prayers, certain worship, or certain deities that will just touch your heart. All of a sudden, you feel like, *oh my God, I know this prayer*, or *I know this Guru*. Like when I saw Babaji's picture, I said, "Oh my God, where do I know him from? He looks so familiar," you have a very deep intimate connection. Everything will start resonating with your soul. The important thing is to start on the spiritual path and if you take one step toward God, he takes a hundred steps towards you. He'll come out, reach out to you. There are many Prayers available like the Chalisas are like 40 prayers and the 108 names. Some people read or write 1,008 names of the mother or of the God that you're close to, like Krishna. There is a Vishnu's Sahasranamam, like thousand names of the Lord Vishnu. There's a Gopal Sahasranamam that has 1,000 names of the Gopal, the baby Krishna.

I am very fond of Gopal from a very young age which means one who protects the cows. Each of the thousand names of Gopal fills your consciousness with the pastimes of Krishna in his childhood and fills you with infinite joy or Parmananda. Then there is the Durga saptashati, the 700 verses for the mother, Durga written by immortal Markandey Rishi. There is Haidakhandi Saptsshati written by Vishnu Dutt Shashtri Ji, and these are 700 verses related to the Divine Mother of Haidakhan where she manifested herself in the compassionate heart of Mahavatar Haidakhan Baba ji.

Babaji says, "Reading and reciting it cures incurable diseases, rids the mind of worries and solves all problems, while an aspirant on the spiritual path attains divine perfection he desires–prosperity in life, worldly happiness, and spiritual peace." Find a prayer that is closer to your heart, and you can take on that prayer and start doing it regularly. You will, with regular dedicated practice, derive the true joy from the prayer, and you will know that you're getting closer and closer to God to your own true self.

The seventh form of devotion is executing the orders of the Lord. So some people have this sentiment that God is everything. I'm just his slave. That's called Dasya Bhava. God will speak to you in your heart as you meditate and get to know him, then he will speak to you through intuition, and you will hear, in the smallest still voice within. He will talk to you, and he will tell you what you should do? And you will know, oh my God, I have to do this because you'll be told in your inner sanctum, in your inner knowing. Some people relate to God as a Master And some people treat God as their friend. Actually, God is everything. God is your mother, father, friend, lover, brothers, sister, everything. But some people like Arjuna in Gita had a relationship with Krishna as his driver, and Draupadi was one of the characters in Mahabharat. She was a goddess. She marched out of a yajna fire. So she always treated Krishna as her friend. Whenever she called on him, he would actually appear to her and save her when she got in trouble with the Kaurava.

There was a time during Mahabharata, there was a royal court of Kauravas who were on the opposite side of Pandavas, and now Kauravas were in power. They were intoxicated with power and money, and they tried to disrobe her right in the middle of a big royal court because they played this game of chess and they cheated, and Draupadi's husband lost. The Kauravas said, "Now we own her. Now she has to come in the middle of this court in front of hundreds of people, and we're going to take her clothes off."

So this one guy, his name is Dushashana, tries to disrobe her and tries to take her Saree off. But she called on Krishna for help, and Krishna started sending unlimited supplies of her Saree. It became unlimited. He started peeling her dress, or Saree, off her body, but it would never end. He finally fell down very exhausted and fainted because he could not remove her Saree anymore.

That is the power of sakha bhav or friendship with God. That means you can develop a relationship with God as your friend because God is closer to you. He's inside of you, but we don't have a relationship with God so that we can call on him when we are in need, and he will come and fulfill whatever we need. That's the worship or developing devotions. We are not alone, but we try to do everything on our own. This devotion is a way to access the power of God. But you have to build a relationship, and through daily practices that we're talking about, you develop that relationship, that connection with God. It becomes real for you and does things for you. Actually, God becomes your servant, and he will do anything for you because many scriptures say that through devotion, you can control the Lord. So you have to develop that relationship.

The last form of devotion is the complete surrender of one's ego. You have to surrender your ego completely, which is a sense of doer-ship that I do everything. Actually, God does everything. There's nothing God does not do because God is in every atom, every subatomic particle. There's nothing that moves without his will. Like Jesus, When he surrendered in the end when he was on a cross, then he told Peter, "If my father wanted to save me, he would send some angels." That's complete surrender to his will. Suppose God wants to save you. He will send an angel, but you have to surrender your ego. You cannot have it your way or His way because only one of you can exist, either you are Him. You surrendered to him. What happens? All His powers are at your disposal because you become one with Him. That's the complete surrender. These are the nine processes or types of devotion.

And there's scripture like *Ramayana* also talks about nine types of devotion. They're very similar to this. In *Ramayana*, Tulsidas talks about the company of the saints as the first type of devotion. Because saints have already developed a loving relationship with God after extensive research in their journey, they have established a connection with God, and that is available to you If you go to the company of the saints. That's why like 500 years ago, Tulsidas said, the first devotion is the company of the saints and Babaji said the same thing in 1984, as he was going into maha samadhi, which is the conscious exit from the body, he said to go to the wise and learn from them because he was not going to be around forever.

Most people who met Babaji had this tremendous realization. With his love and energy, the heart was completely changed. There was a change of consciousness in meeting Babaji, but then they still wanted to continue this life. Babaji said to go to the wise and learn from them. The first step is to know wise people who have already realized God and found God or are trying to search for God. Then you learn from them. In *Ramayana,* saint Tulsidas said, "The second type of devotion is to 'love the stories of God,' like Hanuman, who is the greatest devotee of Lord Rama." Whenever people read the story of Rama, Hanuman will be there. He'll be sitting in the back, and he'll be the first person to arrive and the last person to leave. He's always there. This shows, wherever people are talking about Lord Rama, Hanuman will be there.

So you have to develop passion if you really want to know God, who he is, and what miracles he can do. You want to know more and more about him, and then you want to hear more stories. That's how you deal with the love for God. First, you have to make him real. Then you want to know him, and if you take one step towards him, you will see he will open hundreds of doors for you, and you'll find the stories, information about him, about connecting to God in any form, whether you want to know, father or the mother Krishna Shiva or Jesus. God is only one, but he appears as many, so whatever God is closer to your heart, you want to connect with him through Love. Love is God. There is a saying about Bhakti or devotion. "Bhakti, Bhakta, Bhagvant, Guru, chatur nam vapu ek." Bhakti - Devotion, Bhakta-Devotee, God, and guru, actually, there are four names, but they are one. By devotion, you become one with the guru. First, you become the devotee. Thru devotion, God, Guru, devotee, they all become one.

Basically, there is only one, but we have created a division in our minds. By doing this devotion and complete surrender, you become one with God. That is the best way to connect with God and feel his love in his presence all the time because God is closer to you than you think. Like Jesus when he left said, "I'm always with you." Babaji also, when he left, said, "I'm always with you." He's always with you, but how do you connect with him? How do you feel his presence, his true devotion - through singing, remembering, worship. And these are various ways of doing it. So find a way that suits you, meets your heart's desire, and has a sweet spot for you.

CHAPTER 8

Goddesses

"God simply is. He has no conditions and no limits. He Gives unconditionally. If the door of your heart is closed, he will not come in. He will wait outside, but he will not break in. He is not aggressive because he is love. Love is not aggressive. Love is a constant, uninterrupted and unbreakable flow."

~ Amma- Sri Mata Amritanandmayi Devi

Goddess of wisdom. The goddess of wisdom, knowledge, and arts is known as Saraswati in India and Vedic tradition. Aim is her seed mantra. She is a destroyer of demon consciousness, ignorance, or avidya. You can visualize her sitting on a swan playing a musical instrument called Veena, holding a rosary or mala in one hand and a book in the other hand. There are many prayers to align with her. The first one that I learned when I was like, four or five years old was "Saraswati maya drista Veena pustak Dharini, Hans vahini, samayukta vidya daanam Karotu me." So it's a goddess who sits on a white swan. She holds her Veena, like a guitar, a musical instrument, and a pustak, a book in one hand. A Veena is a long instrument. It resembles a sitar.

It's a string instrument. It has many strings on it, maybe eight. She has both hands on this string, So that is the goddess of the song of creation. Because everything is made from sound. Sound is the building block of the universe.

Right in the beginning was the word, a word we call it sound or nada. She is the mother of the nada, and that nada in the sound is what gives us wisdom. The latest research at Harvard and brain science international now show that every sound activates a different part of our brain. For example, Aum, If you just said *Aum, Aum, Aum*, it lights up the entire brain. That is the goddess of wisdom. She gives you omniscience, meaning knowledge of everything, knowledge of the creation. Her sound is Aim. That's her mantra Aim Saraswatyai Namaha. You ask her for the knowledge before you undertake any projects, and that prayer has been around a long time. I learned it from Swami Ram Deo when I was very young. He has a huge business empire and has several huge naturopathy hospitals. He teaches yoga in India and all over the world. He sells clothes, herbal medicines and teaches different Hatha yoga practices to cure diseases. His turnover is like several billion dollars, like 4,000 crore rupees, which is hundreds of billions of dollars.

The prayer in Sanskrit is :

"SaraSwati namastubhyam.
Varde kamrupini.
Vidyarambha Karisyami
Siddhir bhavatu me sada."
Saraswati, I salute you. I'm starting my study, give me completion, give me success in my undertaking.

The reason for quoting different Sanskrit prayers is that each seed sound activates different parts of your brain, and it gives you that unlimited, awesome intelligence. She's also the goddess of speech and learning. If you want to become an orator or you want to become a singer or writer, you want to pray to Saraswati. She opens your speech, she gives you divine powers, so that you can talk about her creation, she gives you knowledge of the creation. She is full of compassion and loving-kindness. These are different divine attributes of the mind. She's a part of your mind. She purifies your intellect, so you can get to know the light of the God truer self within you. The famous sitar player, Ravi Shankar, played with the Beatles and also lived here in Encinitas near the Self Realization Center, where he used to perform, for a while before he passed away. There was a huge celebration at the Encinitas California SRF Center in his honor when he passed away.

He was a big follower of Saraswati. Now his daughter Anushka Shankar plays Sitar, which is similar to Veena, and he was a follower of Saraswati or Sharda Devi of Maihar, who has a shrine in Maihar, in the state of MP in India. There is a temple of Mother Sharda in Maihar if you seek power or knowledge. This is a very famous temple. You can look that up on the internet. She will give you success in any mission, writing, painting, singing, and if you want to know about creation, she's the goddess. This is a Shakti Peeth or power spot where the necklace of the Divine Mother fell when Shiva was carrying her on his shoulder after she had given her life at the Yagya of her father where Shiva was not invited.

I used to go to a very, very, very small shrine, maybe like four feet by three feet in Varanasi called Saraswati Fatak or Gate of Saraswati. That was right in front of our grandfather's house, where my father grew up. There was just a small hole in the wall. They had just a beautiful face of

Saraswati. The temple was several hundred years old. When I was younger, I used to go there every morning just to look at her face. Her smile would make me very happy. Bismillah Khan was another, a very famous player of Shehnai, a flute that's played at weddings and temples and all auspicious ceremonies. It's a very long flute but uses a lot of breath power. Bismillah khan was a very famous Shehnai player that lived In Varanasi. He used to play for the Lord Kashi Vishwanath every morning till he passed away.

In the eighties, I met him in Berkeley Iskcon temple, and he came down here to play a show. He lived in Banaras. He told me that if you want to write to me, you don't need an address. Just my name and Varanasi, and I will get it. Even if you write Bismillah khan, India, and I will get the letter. That's the power of the grace and blessings of Saraswati. Saraswati is the mother of speech and learning. You'll be drawn to her if you had past life karma and if you want to become an artist and singer now in this life.

Kali:
The next one is a goddess of power, which is also known as a Durga or Kali, and most people are familiar with Swami Ramakrishna, who was a teacher, and Kali used to appear to Him. There's a shrine in Calcutta called Kalighat, still very popular today, visited by millions of people every year.

There is a center, I believe Ramakrishna Mission Center, in Southern California. Kali was also prayed by Paramahansa Yogananda when he was young and living in Calcutta. There's a story in the *Autobiography of a Yogi* where he talks about going to a Kali temple. He went there to pray all day. He stayed there all day, and then mother appeared to him.

Kali Ji also appeared to me, as I had earlier discussed when I was in the Navratri celebration in the Chilianaula after I had done nine nights of the goddess prayers, yagya, pujas, when the goddess's presence is very, very strong she's very accessible. Kali is very much part of the tradition of Gorakhnath. Babaji, some people believe, was in the past Guru Gorakhnath. Babaji established the temple of Kali in Allahabad at the home of Alok Banerjee, a long time devotee and past Chairman of Haidakhandi Samaj. In that temple, Babaji established himself above Kali's statue as Babaji is Mahakala beyond time.

And one of the Babaji's Ashram, in Gujarat, is called manda farm. That's where the Shivratri, the night of Shiva when Shiva is very accessible and Shiva got married to Parvati, is celebrated. The temple that Babaji established in Allahabad in January 1984 before he entered Maha samadhi in February 1984. There was a Kali statue in the Shani temple next to my home, where I grew up in Varanasi. The wife of the priest of the Shani temple who was my nearest neighbor one morning as I was in front of the Kali temple for morning darshan said abruptly with a big smile, "Tore Sange Sange jayinye" meaning she will accompany you from now. She will go everywhere you go, or she will always be with you. I still remember her smiling face as she was smiling when she gave me the blessing of Kali ma.

Kali is very much part of Mahavatar Babaji tradition. Who's Kali? Kali is the divine mother of time. When the whole world goes through dissolution, the whole world is destroyed. At the end of the world, when nothing remains, there is only darkness everywhere. Kali remains. The only thing that remains is the Kali. That's the energy of Kali, so Kali controls everything. In Yoga Vasishtha, Vasishtha tells Rama, the avatar, about how powerful Kali is. Kali is the ultimate transforming power of time that takes us from death to immortality. Kali represents the complete victory of divine overall death and destruction. She removes all the illusions of the mind to discover the eternal presence of our true self that is one in all. Kali holds the Vidyut Shakti, the electrical force of consciousness that is the supreme power. All the goddesses and the entire universe manifests from her electrical force. Kali is endless time, boundless space, and limitless void.

There is a sloka in Durgaspata Shati that says, if you pray to Kali if you worship Kali, she makes you King of all the three lokas or realms, not only the earth but also heaven, as well as the word underneath. That is the power of the Goddess Kali. Most of the universe is not, as you can see, is not light. It is full of darkness. When you look at the sky, or if you look at the stars, there are little stars shining, but then mostly Space is filled with her power Kala Bhairava her consort, which is a Lord of time. Durga Kavach means the shield or armor, which is a prayer to Durga or Kali that was created by Markandey Rishi, who himself was an immortal.

The story behind the Markandey Rishi is that he was born to his father, who was also a Rishi or a Sage, and he prayed to Shiva for the birth of a son. Shiva said, I can give you a son, he'll be very bright, but he will have a very short life, maybe 16 years or so. His father accepted him as a gift from the divine. His father told him that you have a very limited life, so you hang on to Shiva. He will give you a new lease on life. You worship him. If you please, Shiva, then he can give you eternal life. Markandey, from a very young age, started praying to Shiva, and when his time was up, The YamaDuta, or messengers of the god of death called Yama, came, and they wanted to take him away. They said, "Your time is up. You gotta go, you gotta come with us."

So, he hung on to the Shiva lingam, and Marksndey said, "No, I'm not going anywhere."

Then Shiva appeared and said, "No, you cannot take him because he's under my protection, My blessings are with him."

So Shiva gave him the blessing to be immortal. Marksndey Rishi composed this prayer called Durga SaptaShati about the goddess in that there is a prayer called Douga kavacha for the shining armor that protects every single part of your body, provided you read it daily, you can live a hundred years easily. The Kavacha or the shield establishes the goddess, in every part of your body, starting from the forehead, Third Eye, your two eyes, your two ears, your cheeks, the bottom of your ears, shoulders, your lips, your teeth, your throat, and then your Adam's Apple and your palette, and your chin and your tongue. This is a recommended armor or shield. The first time when I was asked to read it, it took me like four hours. You cannot read it because it is in Sanskrit, but you can listen to it on YouTube. The goddess Chandika protects your throat, and your shoulders are protected by Khadgini. She has a sword in her hand. Your arms are protected by Vajra Dharini, a goddess who has a thunderbolt in her hand. Basically, you empower your entire body. You infuse different powers in different parts of your body. Your heart is protected by the Goddess Lalita Devi and your stomach by Shula Dharini, who has a Shula weapon in her hand. Goddess Putna protects your private parts, and Bhagwati, your waste, Kalratri protects your intestines Parvati protects your blood and bones. Your ego, mind, and intellect are protected by the Goddess Dharma Dharini. This is very powerful. In the end, it said that after death, one goes to a place that is rare, inaccessible even to gods. As long as there's the earth with mountains and forests, one who is protected by the armor shield, his family lineage of son and grandson and daughters, great-grandsons, etc., are protected. This incredible power is all power of the mind, but the prayer builds an incredible shield that is created by Markandeya rishi in Markandeya Purana, which is like several thousand pages that talk about the power of these goddesses. I just gave you an example, just by saying the word Durga, destroys all negativity. Actually, the prayer for the mother is from Mahendra Maharaj, who was the disciple of Babaji. He is the one who is responsible for bringing Babaji back into the body in 1970. Mahendra Maharaj had dedicated his whole life in search of Babaji. Babaji had appeared to him when he was a young child on one of his birthdays and gave him some sweets, and then he's evaluated and disappeared in thin air. He spent all his life trying to search for him, and then Babaji appeared to him. in one of his ashrams is called a siddhashram. He went there, and then he appeared to him, and he said, "What do you want, Baba? I just want your blessing." He put both his hands on top of Mahendra Maharaj's head and disappeared again. He walked through this wall where there used to be a gate. He said, "Oh, they closed his gate that used to be here."

Mahendra Maharaj composed a prayer to the mother. "Amba ananda Rupa Cha Atma Alhad Dayini." Oh Mother You Fill me with Supreme joy. Your mercy is the boundless. Mother has the power, but at the same time, she has incredible bliss because she fills the entire space. She is the Supreme Joy. For that is the power of the mother goddess, the Goddess who's our Divine Mother. She is like an ocean of bliss, ocean of compassion and mercy, and also has this incredible power."

This is what Baba ji says about reading and reciting Haidakhandi Saptashati.

> "Reading and reciting it cures incurable diseases, rids the mind of worries and solves all problems while the aspirant on the spiritual path attains the divine perfection he desires–prosperity in life, worldly happiness, and spiritual peace."
>
> ~ Mahavatar Babaji, or. Haidakhan Babaji

Goddess of Abundance

You can get whatever you want by calling on or worshiping Lakshmi, the Goddess of abundance. Her seed mantra is Shreem, and she is golden in color. She sits on a pink Lotus and she's a goddess of heaven called Vaikuntha. She has four arms and, with two arms, holds a lotus flower and two other arms, one arm in blessing, and from the other arm, she showers gold Coins. There are infinite stories about kindness, mercy, and abundant blessings from the mother Lakshmi for meditation. Most famous is the one by Shankaracharya, the great Legend, who started preaching nonduality, ever lived. He used to beg every morning for his food. He went to one poor lady's house, and she said, I don't have anything to give you. He just started praying to the mother goddess of abundance and Gold on the spot and created a hymn or prayer that is now called Kanakadhara stotram. Kanak means gold. Dhara means stream. A stream of gold started pouring into this lady's house after he completed his prayer. He knew that there is a goddess of abundance that is very compassionate, and she has no lack or limitation. When he recited that prayer, this poor lady's house was filled with gold coins from the heavens. Lakshmi's grace and blessings are accessible easily during Venus hora really widely. Some people pray to her on Fridays. Some people pray to her on the full moon day. Some people just chant Shreem Brzee for effortless manifestation, and people have manifested mansions, Cadillacs, private jets just by singing divine praise to the Divine Mother. I just want you to listen to some parts of the Kanakadhara Stotram that Shankaracharya recited and created the shower of gold to give you just the vibration because everything is vibration. You don't have to understand the meaning. The vibration gives you the energy, and then energy turns into matter. The vibration of the sound will create abundance for you. These sounds are very, very powerful. The meaning of the first prayer in the Kanakadhara Stotram is the "dark, flowers in full bloom attract the female beetle, and even so much Lakshmi attracts and finds happiness in the fragrant in dark complexion body of Shri Hari, makes him tingle with joy." Lakshmi is the consort of Vishnu or Shri hari. The one who recites this kind of prayer with faith is blessed with prosperity. That is the goddess of love, plenty, and prosperity. Another famous prayer for wealth is called Shri Suktam. If you do a fire ceremony and read the 16 couplets from Shri Suktam, you will be blessed to live with her grace of non-depleting wealth and prosperity. We will talk about the fire ceremony more as we go through the rituals, but the Shri Suktam basically praises the goddess of abundance for giving you wealth if you have a lack or scarcity consciousness that is keeping you from enjoying the abundance and blessing. The prayer to the mother, Lakshmi, destroys the past karma or Papa called sins. Sin is basically limited thinking. Even though we are abundant, we have no limitations, but because of our limited thinking and past karma, during the thought process, there is scarcity consciousness. Lakshmi will remove our limitations. Lakshmi or Mahalakshmi will remove all your limitations if you pray to her with faith and reverence. There are elaborate fire ceremonies that you can sponsor by trained Vedic priests in India or in the U.S. You can learn how to do it yourself, so there is no lack and limitation. Lakshmi just only wants to give abundance and wants Her children fulfilled.

CHAPTER 9

Gods

"The mind which is matured and enlightened knows that the life of ours is false, imaginary and purely conceptual in nature. Prolonging that perception is meaningless and without any purpose."

~ Sri Raman Maharshi

God of Enlightenment Shiva: Shiva mantras prayers to recite every day the first mantra to recite every day for Shiva is Om Namah Shivaya, and we talked about Om Namah Shivaya earlier Om Namah Shivaya contains Om which is the omnipotent, omnipresent God. Om created everything. Om is the word, in the beginning was the word and in Sanskrit. They call it param Brahma. Om is the god, and the five letters na, ma, shi, va, and ya represent the five elements. In Shiva Purana, Upmanyu, who was the guru of Shri Krishna, tells Krishna, "This Om Namaha Shivaya mantra is the essence of all the Vedas and the Giver of Liberation–it grants liberation. In the letter Om Devadi Dev Mahadev is present. Devadi Dev is the god of all the gods that know everything. Mahadev himself is present in the Om Namah Shivaya mantra. Subtle cosmos called Ishaan etc., are present, and Shiva always resides in this mantra. The one who recites it becomes Niskalanka, which means he becomes blemishless, all his sins are destroyed, all his limitations are destroyed, and he crosses the ocean of the world and gets liberated." So this is a very powerful mantra. The five letters represent five elements: earth, water, fire, air, and space. Na represents the Earth element. A lot of people meditate on the lower part of their body with Na sound like your feet, your shins, your calves, your knees, and thighs. Ma is this second letter that represents the element water. Water element fills your stomach and your navel and all the way up to your chest. Shi represents the fire element. You can visualize the entire chest, heart, and lungs full of golden light or the fire element. Va represents the element of air that fills your throat chakra and your shoulders, and then Ya is the space or ether element. The space element occupies higher parts of your brain, your eyes, and ears. Shiva's mantra contains all elements and the god of the gods Devadhi Dev Mahadev, even the cosmos. Everything is contained in this five-letter mantra. The first thing is to do is recite Om Namah Shivay. The proper way to do it is Japa, which is repeating the name of the god or mantra. Before you get into Japa, you should take a shower, get fresh, and put on clean clothing and find a clean place, where nobody will be disturbing you, and then you engage yourself in Japa. There are five different processes or procedures for doing Japa. The first one is called Vachik. It means just repeating Om Namah Shivaya, Om Namah Shivaya. You keep doing that, or you can sing Om Namah Shivay, Om Namah Shivay. What you get with the first type of Japa, is it has benefits equal to a one-time number of Japa. If you do Japa a hundred and eight times, you get the benefit of a hundred and eight mantras Japa, but if you do, Upanshu Japa, which is done quietly, it is a hundred times more powerful. It's called upanshu which means, you don't say it out loud. You repeat it in your mind. and if you want to go even quieter, which is you just think in your mind that you are saying the mantra and nobody will hear it, only you will know it's called Manas

Japa, which is a thousand times more powerful And if you Add Aum before and after the mantra it is a hundred thousand times more powerful. Last but not least is you do Japa with meditation with Dhyan in the mantra that means you visualize Om Namah Shivaya. Look at the words and meditate on them while you're doing Japa. It's even a thousand times more powerful. There are stages of Japa as you go. As you practice, it becomes more and more powerful. The pranayama should be done before we go into Japa in order to quieten the Mind. There are many techniques of controlling the breath and doing the pranayama before we do the Japa.

The simple way to do pranayama is you take your breath from one nostril like, for example, from the left side, close the right nostril, and breathe through the left. You can say Aum 18 times, and you keep taking the breath in and then you hold the breath In the middle of your forehead where your third eye is, and you look at your third eye, and you say Om 18 times, and then you exhale from the right nostril while you say Om 18 times. Then you breathe again from the right nostril and keep chanting Om 18 times, and then you hold again in the middle of the forehead where the third eye is, and you chant Om 18 times, and you let go from the left nostril. Again you repeat this process three times. Inhale from the left side, holding in the middle. You imagine you're taking a breath in, and you're filling up the lungs like a balloon and then holding it for a while and then letting it out through the right nostril. Again breathe in from the right nostril. Hold it in the middle of the forehead and let it out through the left, and you repeat that three times. This is the process given in the Devi Bhagavatam. It is also practiced by Babaji and given by him to his devotees in Herakhan. It is very powerful because it immediately stops the mind. The mind becomes calm so that you are ready to engage in a deeper meditation or in Japa. The pranayama should be done before you do Om Namah Shivaya. The other very powerful mantra of Shiva is called Maha Mrityunjaya, or victory over death mantra, which gives you immortality and victory over death. You can Google it and find it on YouTube, and you can find the tune you like, but I will give you the words and the sound, and just meditating on the sound Of the Maha Mrityunjaya mantra destroys all negativity. All chronic diseases are eliminated, and it gives you perfect health. You should just start with doing Japa a hundred and eight times. Babaji has told me that I can do 11 malas every morning. Because one time I wanted to know, when I heard about this mantra from Swami Chidanand in San Francisco, *how many times should I do it?* I was asking in my mind and Babaji appeared to me in a dream and he said you can do eleven malas because it gives you victory or death and basically gives you the realization of your Immortal nature. You are Shiva immortal being living in this mortal body and that is achieved by Mahamrityunjaya mantra. "Tryambakam Yajamahe Sugandhim pushti Vardhanam urva rukamiva bandhanan mrityor mukshiya Maamritat." I'm going to tell you its meaning. This mantra is available online. You can find different melodies, you can sing or you can quietly do Japa. If you have a Mala, like a rosary, you can repeat it a hundred eight times. Tryambakam is the name of the Shiva with three eyes. This is a prayer to the Shiva who has three eyes and the third eye is the pineal gland which is located slightly above and behind the pituitary gland. There's a pineal gland which is in the middle of the brain. It looks like a small pine cone as well. It is called the pineal gland and actually looks like a third eye, so you can meditate on the third eye. Tryambakam yaja mahe means I prayed to the Shiva with three eyes. Sugandhim pushti vardhanam means just like a cucumber on a tree falls when it's ripe Mrityor mukshiya maamritat means release me from death into immortality. You free me from the bondage and liberate me, give me freedom from death. Mrityu means death and mukti means liberation. Give me liberation from death or mortality. Another visualization you can do is see Shiva holding two pots of nectar pouring it on himself.

Then there is another famous Shiva mantra or long chanting called Chamakam Namakam which is done with an Abhishek or hydration ceremony. This is an elaborate ritual. It does not take that long, once you get used to this as daily worship before you engage in meditation or pranayama. First I take a shower I go down to my temple that I have set up and I do the Abhishek hydration ritual or Shodashopachara Pooja using 16 of these steps. It is very similar to inviting a guest to your family and entertaining them. First, you send the invite. When the guest shows up you offer him a seat, then you offer him water to wash his feet and hands and then some water to rinse his mouth. Then you give him a bath. As I write this, I am reminded of the rule of St. Benedict on devotion to hospitality. "Brothers and sisters: Let mutual love continue. Do not neglect hospitality. For through it some have unknowingly entertained angels," Hebrew 13:1.

What you have to do is obtain a small Shiva lingam that you can buy on Amazon. It's very inexpensive and you just search for Shiva lingam. Once you get it, you put the Shiva lingam in a dish then you are going to offer him a bath. You can use just water to start with, but most people in ritual bathing use five ingredients: milk, yogurt, honey ghee, and sugar. You can see this online in all the Shiva temples in India. They do a very elaborate rudrabhishek hydration ceremony with the five Nectars. You start with water, then you pour milk, yogurt, ghee, or clarified butter and honey.

The last thing is sugar. These are called five Nectars and Shiva puran gives you a very elaborate description of the benefit of using these Ingredients. It destroys the negativity from your life and gives you sweetness in relationships, gives you prosperity and no disease. There are basically the five elements themselves we are offering to Shiva. On top of that, you can find the chanting for rudrabhishek, praise of Shiva, in 158 songs that are called Chamakam which talks about the greatness of Shiva.

If you have more time, especially on Mondays and on pradosham, which is the 13th moon one hour before sunset, is the power time that you can use to remove a lot of Karma and negatively just by offering the panchamrit or the five Nectars while you chant Om Namah Shivaya. If you want to get more benefit you can hire a Vedic priest to do the rudrabhishek to remove negativity and root out bad karma.

For the even greater benefit of humanity, I sponsored an Ati rudrabhishek being conducted by 11x11x11 priests chanting 11 times for 11 days to end the pandemic. In our home, we can do a simple rudrabhishek by just offering water, milk, yogurt, honey, ghee, or clarified butter and sugar. You can say "Panchamrutham Samarpayami" or you can chant or sing "Om Namah Shivaya." You can play the rudrabhishek mantra that is about half an hour long. Shiva is extremely pleased with that and he grants all your desires, whatever wishes you have are fulfilled. That is the abhishekam or ritual bathing. After bathing you dry the lingam and then you offer him clothes to wear just like you would if you have a guest at home. You ask him if he'd like to take a bath and then you have for him new clothes to wear. We offer him yagyopavit, a sacred thread you can buy online. It is like the six or seven threads that have no joints. It is a continuous loop that you put around

Shiva and then after that, you offer the perfume with Sugandhim samarpayami. Then you offer him some Chandan, which is sandalwood paste and Kumkum. Then you offer him incense and then we offer him a light or deep which is a lamp made by ghee and then you offer him Tambulum of Betel Leaf, which is traditionally used after the food and then finally you offer light. This completes the 16-step ritual. If it is too much to do in the beginning, you can just start with water and offer Chandan, Sandalwood paste and Kumkum. The three things will complete the ritual and what's most important in all these rituals is not the technique. It is your mindset and your heart.

I want to quote here because you're doing that for Shiva who is your own higher self, your soul, but you cannot offer it to the Shiva whose inside your heart. This symbol of Shiva lingam was created after Shiva appeared as a linga or column of light. There was a discussion among the three Gods, the Brahma, the creator, Shiva the destroyer, and Vishnu, who is the protector, who is the greatest among three. Shiva himself appeared as an infinite column of light and Brahma went searching the first end and he could not find it. They went for thousands of years because he was infinite and had no end. Brahma lied and he said I have seen the end so that's when Shiva created the fierce form of Kala Bhairava. Brahma had five heads. Kala Bhairava cut his fifth head just with his nail. The head got stuck to Kala Bhairava's hand and Kala Bhairsva traveled all over the world and when he ended up in Banaras and took a bath in the Ganges there, the head of Brahma fell off from his hand. On that spot still today there is the famous Temple of Kala Bhairava in Banaras.

Shiva is everywhere, omnipresent as light and the symbol of Shiva lingam represents that infinite linga or column of light, and we are trying to please him with this ritual which is a very mysterious process. But your love is what unfolds the mystery of the soul or mystery of the god or Shiva no other than your own soul. Most people don't know that the same Shiva resides in every one of us. Actually, there is only one soul and is full of eternal bliss or Nityananda and Paramananda is the other name for it.

Rumi who had some experience of self-love talks about love and what he says here. "To whom the mystery of love is revealed exists no longer. What happens? you disappear, you vanish into love. Just like if you place before the sun a burning candle and watch its brilliance disappear before that blaze and that candle no longer exists. It is transformed into light." That's what you are trying to do with this infinite column of light that is in front of you and you're trying to disappear your mind and your five senses into it. That's why these elaborate rituals are created so that you lose yourself. Then you become one, you transform into light just like Rumi said it.

So let me repeat, Rumi said, "The person to whom he unveils the mystery of love no longer exists, but he vanishes into Love. Place before the sun a burning candle and watch its brilliance disappear before that blaze the candle exists No longer. It is transformed into light." That's our goal. We are like anyone who gets transformed into light. Just like we talked about Kabir earlier, he disappeared into light or Jesus, disappeared in light, and then reappeared, just to show that I'm not going anywhere. This is a process. What is the prerequisite? It is also called oneness. You are controlling the mind. The prerequisite for this process of controlling your mind is taught by Mahendra Maharaj, who was instrumental in bringing Babaji Back in a human form. Babaji stayed here only for 14 years, but he walked among us, not as Jesus appeared for a short time, but Babaji appeared, and he stayed in his Himalayan place, which he called Herakhan. He stayed there for 14 years.

What Mahendra Maharaj says is the most important–faith. one should have faith in his guru and the guru is the one who takes you from duality into oneness with the infinite. Guru is in between you, your five senses or five elements, and the Supreme Being, who is infinite. Guru removes all your limitations from limited being, you become unlimited, but you have to have faith in your guru. After faith comes what we call Sadhana. What we're talking about is practice. This is a practice you're going to develop and are you going to keep on doing it until you achieve your goal, which is oneness with the Shiva. The practice, again, has two fundamental processes and in Sanskrit, it is called Sahan and Sumiran. Sahan means tolerance. You have to have tolerance and forgiveness while you're doing this practice because it takes a long time. Sumiran is the second part of the Sadhana. Sumiran also means remembering God at all times. Sahana suggests tolerance, and it also requires patience. Tolerance, patience, and perseverance give you practice with faith and perseverance, then you will know the truth, and the truth will set you free. That is, in a nutshell, our practice. You need to develop that. You can build and incorporate into your schedule, into your lifestyle. I'm able to do that every morning and evening before I start my day, And when I finish my day, the end of the day around sunset. Then I do the evening session to clear up my mind and again. Do my Japa and then follow that by an hour of not only light offering but also singing. As we talk about rituals, I will talk more about the Arti.

Hanuman:

Now let's go to my most favorite god, Hanuman, who is a symbol of unshakeable faith, courage, and devotion. For him nothing is impossible. Hanuman is called the impossibility buster. You've probably seen Hanuman as Monkey God. He's usually seen carrying a mountain in one hand and he has a mace or a club in one hand called Gada and his color is red and he's shown with a third eye, or sometimes you see him flying with the two brothers Ram and Lakshman on his two shoulders. There is a temple with Hanuman carrying a mountain built by Ramdas, devotee of Neem Karoli Baba in Taos, New Mexico. There is a monkey god or Hanuman carrying a mountain.

There are many stories about Hanuman. Hanuman means one who has killed his pride. One of his names is Pawansut, son of the wind god. He is called an impossible buster because he has incredible power. Hanuman is an incarnation of Shiva. Shiva created him to go and serve Rama when Rama was on Earth's plane. One of the prayers for Hanuman in Ramayana is:

"Pawan tanay bal pawan samana.
Buddhi Vivek vigyan nidhana,
Kaun so Kaj Kathin jag mahi
Jo nahi hot tat tum pahi."

What that means is, *you are the son of the wind, someone who has incredible strength like wind, and you are the reservoir of intelligence discrimination and immense strength. There's nothing for you that is impossible or hard. What is it that you cannot do? There is nothing that you cannot do.* We talked about it earlier. But the mountain you see him carrying has life-giving herbs, and that's what was needed because when there was a battle with Ravana in Sri Lanka and actually Meghnath, one of the sons of Ravana, had used a weapon on Lakshman, the brother of Lord Rama who became unconscious. There was a Vaidya or Indian medicine man called Sukhain. He said, the only way we can bring him back to life, is we need to bring this herb that's available on the Dronagiri mountains, up in the Himalayas, and they were in the southern part of India. The doctor said he has to be given that remedy of herbal medicine sanjivani buti before sunrise tomorrow. Hanuman flew because he is the son of wind and he flew with an incredible speed and some scientists have estimated the speed is like a thousand six hundred kilometers an hour, almost like a plane. He can go so fast and he has immense strength. He went up to the mountain. He could not figure out which herb to get because they all look the same to him. This herb was supposed to have a little light. The doctor told him to pick up the herb that has a light. The mountain was all lit up at night and he could not figure it out. Hanuman said I'm going to just take this whole mountain. He flew back south with the mountain and Lakshman got his life back. That is what is available to you through devotion, through prayer through love.

Wherever there are people talking about Ram, singing to Ram or Ramayana because he's there as he has totally dedicated and devoted his life to Rama. I'm going to just say Jai Sri Ram so that you can feel the vibration and from that, you can get the vibration of Hanuman energy and for him nothing is Impossible. When you have impossible tasks, you cannot do it yourselves, you turn to Hanuman and he'll accomplish the task for you. The most popular prayer for Hanuman is called Hanuman Chalisa 40 couplets in praise of Hanuman and was composed by Tulsidas about 500 years ago. Actually, in those days there was a Muslim ruler in India named Akbar. He heard that Tulsidas had all these powers.

He called Tulsidas to his palace and said, "I want to see Ram, I want to see Hanuman, I want to have a Darshan."

So Tulsidas said, "That's not possible. You have to have love in your heart. You have to have devotion. Then they will appear in front of you or not appear. I cannot do that." Akbar kept Tulsidas in captivity. Tulsidas started just remembering Hanuman and calling on Hanuman. How great Hanuman is. That's when he composed this Hanuman Chalisa. He starts with "Sri Guru charan saroj Raj Nij man Mukur Sudhar. …….Bal Budhi Vidya Deh Mohi Harshu Klesh Vikar."

I remember first my Guru. I remember I asked him to give me strength, Buddhi means intelligence, and Vidya means knowledge and to remove my agony and pain. As he started singing this prayer to Hanuman, thousands of monkeys just started walking toward that palace in New Delhi where he was kept in captivity and they just covered that palace. All these monkeys, thousands of them, entered and surrounded the palace. When Akbar, the ruler, saw that he was scared and he surrendered to Hanuman. Then he let Tulsidas go. That's how the Hanuman Chalisa was created. You can find a recording online and there are millions of people like a hundred million people who have watched Hanuman Chalisa. You can see Hanuman Chalisa online by many different singers. You can find the one that you like and learn and get to know Hanuman Chalisa as it is sung every day in Babaji's ashram, Neem Karoli Babaji's ashram in India and in the U.S. as we talked about earlier, here in New Mexico, and also there is some ashram in Germany, everywhere worldwide. They are millions of followers of Hanuman.

There are two most famous temples of Hanuman, where a strong presence of Hanuman can still be felt today and where he's alive like it is his home. One of the oldest temples is in Ayodhya where Rama the avatar lived and ruled for like ten thousand years. There's a temple for Hanuman called Hanuman Garhi and they have a live broadcast of the Arti. You can have the Darshan of the Hanuman at the temple from your living room without leaving the comfort of your home. That's one Hanuman Temple. The other one is Varanasi, where I was born. The temple of Hanuman is called Sankat Mochan Hanuman, one who can get you out of trouble. Sankat means trouble, mochan means the one who liberates you. When you get in trouble, you call on him, and he'll get you out of trouble. The story of how this temple was built goes that when Tulsidas was writing the Ramayana in Banaras, he heard that Hanuman comes there where the story of RAM or Ramayana is recited.

In those days, 500 years ago, there was a place called Nichi Baag where they used to recite the story of Rama in Sanskrit from Valmiki Ramayana. There an old man will come before everybody else. He would stay through the whole program and leave only after everyone leaves. Tulsidas figured out this was Hanuman. One day as Hanuman was leaving Tulsidas followed him. As he was near the forest at the end of town Tulsidas grabbed his feet and said, "I know who you are. Please tell me where I can find my Ishta Dev Prabhu Shri Ram. I want to have his darshan." Hanuman was in the form of an old man who did not want to admit that he was Hanuman, the powerful Monkey God. But Tulsidas followed him through the entire city, and as they were getting into the forest that was the end of the city of Banaras. Finally, Hanuman appeared to him and he said, you can go to Chitrakoot, that's where you'll find Lord Ram. That's where this temple is built, where Monkey God Hanuman appeared and gave darshan to Tulsidas. This temple is very close to Banaras Hindu University where I got my first degree in engineering. The temple is very close to the entrance of the university, and a lot of students regularly make a stop there on a weekly basis. Whenever I could on my way to school or back, I would visit the temple of Sankat Mochan Hanuman on Tuesdays and Saturdays. Thousands of people line up for darshan and get their wishes fulfilled. Last year when I was in India with my wife, we both went to the temple and had a darshan at the Sankat Mochan Hanuman temple which is very famous worldwide. His name is also mentioned in Hanuman Chalisa. "Sankat se Hanuman chudave, man Kram vachan dhyan jo lave." Whoever prays to Hanuman with the mind, action, and speech gets out of trouble.

If you have more time and patience than you can read, Sunderkand to build a relationship with Hanuman Ji. Sunderkand is one chapter in Ramayana dedicated to Hanuman, how he flew to Lanka and helped Lakshman and Rama find his wife that was kidnapped and how Hanuman was instrumental in helping Rama defeat Ravana and his army. There are many incredible stories of Hanuman in Sunderkand, the most beautiful chapter in Ramayana. You can listen to it on YouTube and there is an English translation of the Ramayana available. You can read the whole Ramayana or read the chapter on Sundarkand and it will strengthen your devotion. Hanuman does appear to people who are very dedicated to him. He did appear to my mother in Fremont when we were living there. One of my younger brother's sons, who was like five years old, passed away, and when my mom heard that news, she was totally devastated and she was crying like crazy. How could this happen? Then we called Muni Raj Ji, who was our guru at the time, and we had her on the phone talking to Muniraj Ji. And my mom was telling me several months after the call that as he was talking, all of a sudden she saw Hanuman appear right there in our living room. She said, "I closed my eyes and I could see him. His form occupied the whole room, from the floor all the way up to the ceiling. I closed my eyes, and I could still see him. I opened my eyes to see him." Hanuman does appear and there are hundreds of stories on miracles of Hanuman. You can find them online, people who report their experiences, of how Hanuman has helped them.

So Hanuman is very active in Kaliyuga right now actually when he was in Lanka and that is the story in Sunderkand, mother Sita, the wife of Rama is Jagdamba the goddess. She gave him a boon that he can bless you with eight types of supernormal powers called Ashta Siddhis and Nava Nidhi–nine types of treasures.

The eight Siddhis are:

1. Anima: the ability to reduce one's size
2. Mahi-ma: the ability to expand one's size
3. Garima- the ability to make one heavy
4. Laghima- the ability to make one lightweight
5. Prapti: Acquire anything from anywhere
6. Prakamya- Satisfy any desire
7. Ishtva- The ability to duplicate oneself
8. Vas tva- The ability to dominate all

Hanuman's various adventures glorified in Sundarkand reveal that he has these supernormal powers. That's why he can become very small or very large–lift a mountain and fly in the air.

There are eight types of superpowers like making us all very small and disappearing. Prapti is getting what you want. He can give you those supernatural powers and nine types of treasures, all those things. Seek you first the Kingdom of God and his righteousness, and all those things will be added onto you. All those things, anything you want, can be obtained with the devotion of Hanuman. He lives in all four epochs. He's been living, and he was on the earth and he will remain on the earth. No matter what happens he will be there for millions of years. As long as the earth remains, Hanuman will be there. Hanuman will give you courage and strength and do the impossible. But you must learn how to reach out to him and learn the best way to do it.

Kala Bhairava:
Now we'll talk about the God of time and space Kala Bhairava. I mentioned earlier how he was created. He is the fierce form of Shiva himself. Kala Means time. He manufactures time, not only for earth, for all the galaxies. His mantra is Kala Bhairavaya Namaha and there's a temple. In Varanasi that is very famous. He destroys the time for you, and that means the time or kala has no effect on you. Kala Bhairava is a protector, you'll find him in every temple of the goddess, you see him as a guard called Kshetra pal. He will not let the evil spirit enter into your home or into your place of worship wherever you install him. I have a Kala Bhairava statue that came to me from one of the Babaji centers in Nebraska.

The seed mantra for Kala Bhairava is bum bum or Bum bum bum batukaya Namah. That's his other mantra. There is a mantra in the Shiva sutra called Udyamo Bhairava. Shastri Ji used to sing 108 names of Kala Bhairava. That is also sung in the guru Gorakh nath ashrams. The first part is "Om Kar Kalit Kapal, kundali, dand pani, Tarun timir, vyal yagyoPaviti. Kratu samay saparya vighn vicched hetu jaytu. Batuknath siddhi dah Sadhakanam." I pray to the young batuk nath dand pani who has a skull in his hand and wears a snake as a yagyopavit or thread. I pray to him to remove the obstacles in gaining Siddhi perfection or supernormal powers.

There is also a prayer to Kala Bhairava composed by Adi Shankaracharya himself called Ashtakam which means eight prayers to Kala Bhairava or Kalabhairava Ashtakam. It says that Kala Bhairava can give you eight siddhis and incredible fame. "Ashta siddhi dayakam, Vishal kirti dayakam." And destroys sins accrued while living in Kashi.

Hanuman, Kala Bhairava, and Kali are part of Babaji's army and also part of the guru Gorakh Nath community. He fulfills our desire; he is very kind to his devotees. He protects his devotees and since he can destroy the Kala or Time itself. Babaji looked like a 16 or 17-year-old when he appeared in a cave in Haidakhan in 1970, but his age was several thousand years. Leonard Orr who spent a lot of time with Babaji told me his age was 9000 years. Babaji used to take a bath every afternoon in the river Gautami Ganga and some devotees were invited to bathe him and wash him afterward. Leonard told me that when he was giving a bath, he got an opportunity to touch his skin which was soft like a newly born baby's skin. As Leonard was admiring his soft skin Babaji said to him, "This is a very old body. The body is 9000 years old."

Some people say that Babaji is Kala Bhairava himself as he could appear in more than one place at the same time. Just by praying to Kala Bhairava will protect you and fulfill your desire and give you a youthful appearance. Babaji says Kala Bhairava appears in the fire. When you do the fire ceremony Kala Bhairava will appear, and he will protect you. He rides a black dog. All those people you see right now who have a black dog are Kala Bhairava devotees. You can search Kala Bhairava online and find more pictures. There's a Kala Bhairav Temple in Ujjain, in Nepal Kathmandu–the world-famous Kala Bhairava temple in Varanasi. Kala Bhairava is the only God that you can offer alcohol to and I heard that in Ujjain Kala Bhairava temples you can see alcohol flowing freely outside the temple where you can see the dogs in the night drunk in the street.

The dark form of Kala Bhairava is Related to Kali and the story goes when Kali was very angry like she is right now, she was destroying everything. So Kala Bhairava took the form of a little boy and he laid down in front of her. She was marching forward, killing the demons, with both hands, and stepped on Batuk Bhairav when she saw Batuk Bhairav, the little boy, in front of her, her tongue came out of her mouth and then her motherly love came out and then she stopped the killing.

There are eight different types of Bhairava and there are eight temples in Banaras. Because Kala Bhairava is not only in Banaras–he's everywhere. The best time to praise Kala Bhairava is on Sunday between 6 and 8 p.m. A lot of people go to the Kala Bhairava Temple on Sundays. A lot of people offer alcohol to Kala Bhairava on Sunday. Kala Bhairava is there for you and he will protect you from dark forces and fulfill all your desires.

Vishnu:
Vishnu Is the god of prosperity, luxury, abundance, and wealth. Krishna is one of the Avatars of Vishnu and so was Ram. Actually, Vishnu had ten avatars from the beginning of time. Every time the Dharma declines, Krishna says in Bhagavad Geeta, "yada yada Hi Dharmasya glanir bhavati bharata." That means whenever the Dharma declines, I take a form and appear to protect the dharma to protect the holy land and kill

the wicked people. That's the story of Vishnu and he appeared as Krishna and destroyed the wicked King Kansa, his mother's brother and then he destroyed Putna when he was very young. That is the role of Vishnu. He protects his devotees. You can find the form that appeals to you because we all have lived millions of lives, and we had a relationship with the divine in many forms in previous lives.

There was a Narsingh avatar when he appeared as a lion-man god that is still very, very powerful, very alive and worshipped daily in Mayapur at the Hare Krishna headquarter. There's a big Temple of Narsingh Bhagwan in Banaras next to the Annapurna Temple. There is the mantra for narasimha: Ugram Verram Maha Vishnu Jwalantam Sarvato mukham, narsingh bheeshansm, bhadram mrituor mrityu namamyaham.

I want to tell you the story about Prahlad who was a young boy like a five six-year old devotee of Vishnu, and he used to say the name of Vishnu Narayan, Narayan all the time. His father was a king. His name was Hiranyakashipu and he was very against Vishnu because he thought he was the most powerful man. He said, "I am the god. I am everything. Nobody's bigger than me. Why do you pray to Vishnu? Who is Vishnu? What can he do?, I'm the king. I'm the God."

So Prahlad said, "No, no, no, no, no. Vishnu Narayan is everywhere. He can do anything Narayan always protects his devotees." Hiranyakashipu tries to kill Prahlad, his own son, tries to throw him from the Mountain, tries to set him on fire and nothing happens to him. He came out unharmed. Hiranyakashipu got very mad at Prahalad. He said, "Why do you keep on calling, repeating the name of my enemy. I am the greatest." And he said, "Where is your Narayan? Show me. Do you think he's in this pillar?" He was in his royal court and there was a huge pillar.

Prahalad said, "Yeah, of course. Not only is the Narayan in this pillar, he's hidden in every pillar." The reason Hiranyakashipu was so powerful was that he had prayed to Brahma the Creator. Then he got a boon that nobody could kill him, neither man, nor woman, neither in the day or night, with any weapon and neither inside the home or outside. Brahma said, "Okay I give you the boon. Now, nobody, no man, or woman will be able to kill you. No weapon will be able to kill you. You're not to be killed inside the home or outside the home." What happened? He was challenging Prahlad, his own son. Prahlad said, "Yeah, God is here. Vishnu is here in the Pillar." Hiranyakashipu ran across the hall. He took his club like a mason. He hit that pillar and the pillar shattered and there was a loud thunder noise in the room and Lord Narasimha appeared like the flame and filled the entire space. He had the form of a lion and a man because the boon was that no man or woman can kill him but he was a lion-man God and he has sharp nails and so he used his nails and he did not use any weapon. Then he carried Hiranyakashipu to the threshold of their house so they would be either inside the house or outside and then put Hiranyakashipu on his thighs because he said I cannot be killed anywhere, either on Earth or in the sky. Narasimha put him on his lap. He used his nails to rip him open, and then he killed Hiranyakashipu. That is the power of Vishnu, how he protects his devotees. If you have faith in Vishnu Then he'll protect you whether you pray to Vishnu as a Nara Simha or Krishna or Ram. There are so many forms He appeared in the past.

Hayagreeva is a horse-faced avatar in the early days. But the most recent avatar was Krishna, and you can see how Krishna performed miracles when he was very young. He killed a demon named Putna when he was like a baby because she tried to give him poison. She put poison on her nipples and tried to feed Krishna and so he killed Putna. He had been killing demons all his life. That is the role to destroy the negativity and protect the devotees. Some Krishna devotees sing Hare Krishna, Hare Krishna, Krishna, Krishna, Hare Hare or Vishnu sahasranama thousand names of Vishnu if you don't know Sanskrit. You don't need to know how to read it. You can just listen to the sound vibration. You can just put a tape on and just listen to the thousand and names of the Vishnu. Vishnu Sahashra naam, that's how it goes. "Yasya Smarana matrena Janm Sansar Bandhanat vi Muchyate Namastasye Vishnave Prabhu vishnave." So what that means is just by remembering him like what we are doing now, all the bondages of the world are destroyed. I salute Vishnu. So just by saying Vishnu Vishnu or just by remembering him just remembering the story of Narasimha or playing his mantra Ugram veeram maha vishnu or simply imagining a giant form of a man with the lion face and huge nails who destroys the negativity and will protect you. Of course, the Bhagavad Gita that came out of the mouth of Krishna on the battlefield tells you how to live. We talked about many quotes from the Gita, but you can select a chapter like chapter 12. It is very popular because it's on Bhakti yoga. You can read that, and in it Krishna says, "One who sees me everywhere, one who sees all in me for him. I am never lost nor is lost to me." So the simplest way to see Vishnu or Krishna is to see him in everyone. Everybody you meet. There's only him. Only Krishna sees all in him, sees everything in him and sees him everywhere. Then he'll never be lost for you. So you have to develop that relationship with that mindset, with faith and reverence.

There is a temple in the South in Tirupati called Balaji Temple and it is a world-famous Vishnu temple. I'll tell you about a few famous temples of Krishna or Vishnu that you can visit if you are ever in India, or he will call you if you are someone who has spent time with him in the past lives. My wife and I went after a long time to Tirupati Balaji Temple, which has an annual revenue of a billion or several billion dollars and people from all walks of life travel there and there are long lines. People wait eight hours, 10 hours, 16 hours. Sometimes 24 hours a day just to get inside the temple. When we flew, I think in 2015 we took a direct flight from Seattle on Korean Airlines and landed directly in Chennai, and we took a taxi straight to the temple. There were no lines, all the gates were open to us and we were just totally surprised by the miracle all the gates were open. We were able to get in and out of the temple within a couple of hours–that's a miracle. Really think of him, and he thinks of you. You can go visit Tirupati and you can see the Balaji temple online. You can have his picture in your home if you want a lot of wealth or Prosperity. You can have a statue of Balaji. You can find that online also. There is a famous temple in Vrindavan, of course, that's where Krishna was born. Some of my relatives actually own or they're the Seva adhikari or the priest in the Vrindavan temple called Banke bihari Temple. There is a Live Krishna with a dark complexion with Radha and he is very alive and they open the curtain only for a few minutes because there are stories that he will run away. He ran away with one of the princes of Rajasthan. He's very alive and he answers people's prayers and people see Krishna all the time. There are so many stories about Krishna from vrindavan. You must visit Dwarka. Krishna lived in Dwarka as a king after he grew up. He spent his time in Dwarka, which is on the west coast of India in Gujarat. My wife and I went and spent some time there.

There's a Temple called Dwarkadhish, a huge Temple and you can see Krishna as the king because he ruled there over a hundred years in Dwarka so you can see, touch, feel his presence there. Of course, Ram was born in Ayodhya, which is in UP, Uttar Pradesh. I talked about the Hanuman Garhi Temple there. You can go to a temple called Janm Bhumi where Ram was born and those are the two Birth places of Rama and Krishna There's a temple which is called Jagannath temple located In Orissa. Jagannath means Lord of the universe. The Jagannath Temple is very famous. There's a lot of stories associated with it and the three deities.

CHAPTER 10

Mantras rituals and meditations

"Even kings and emperors with heaps of wealth and vast dominion can not compare with an ant filled with the love of God."

~ Guru Nanak

Mantras are subtle sounds and the greatest gift of our Rishis of ancient times. It is the greatest gift to humanity to control the mind because with the mantra you can control your mind. You can watch your mind and you can achieve everything. Mantras are the subtle sound that the Rishis have heard in deep meditation that comes from the cosmos or different galaxies. The mantra is the subtle sound and is the building block of the universe. Everything is made up of the word like, in the beginning, was the word and word became flesh and dwelt among us. The word is actually sound and sound is the mantra. There are mantras for everything. You can get whatever you want to accomplish. If you cannot do that with the rational mind, you can do that with the midbrain which is called the third eye. The sound of the shakti activates the power of the Kundalini shakti within you. The energy that is dormant becomes active by the power of the mantra. That's how powerful the mantra is. There are simply thousands and thousands of mantras, but any sound that we can use to control the mind or watch the mind is a mantra. The mantra is what gives you the ability to have control.

You become the witness of your mind, and then you're able to control it and direct it to get what you want. You are the controller and creator of your destiny, provided you keep your mind in control. Mantra gives you the power to control your mind and then your destiny and build a life the way you want and realize your true nature and eventually become free from this cycle of going around the world, coming and going, so you get free from the rebirth, you get liberated. The simple, most profound mantra is Om Namaha Shivaya, the mantra given at the beginning of the creation to humanity. Just by repeating Om Namaha Shivaya continuously, everything can be achieved, including victory over death, liberation and immortality. Everything can be achieved just by simply repeating the mantra Om Namah Shivay. In Shiva purana, there is a mention of the guru of Shri Krishna named Upmanyu. Upmanyu told Krishna, "Om Namah Shivay is the essence of all the vedas, and it is a giver of liberation because Devadhi Dev Mahadev himself is present in this mantra, and the one who repeats, this mantra becomes immortal and crosses the ocean of the world."

We talked about this earlier. I think there are five ways of repeating the mantra. Some people say that ten times or one hundred and eight times. But mantra, you are supposed to repeat constantly. The easiest way to repeat the mantra is to break it down in five parts. If you're not familiar with the mantra Om Namah Shivay, it also contains the five elements. Na represents the earth element, MA represents the water element, Shi represents the Fire element, VA represents the air element and YA represents the space element. everything is made of the five elements. Babaji had control over the five elements through the power of this mantra. You can also have any name or any sound as a mantra. Some people say Shivay, Shivay, Shivay. Then started repeating the same name on one track quietly in your mind. When you just think about the mantra all the time and you can listen to the sound of the mantra or Naad in your mind that your mind is now focused on the mantra, your sphere of the mantra, but you're also watching all your thoughts and so it gives you that power.

There are mantras for achieving health, becoming disease-free, or there is a mantra for achieving unlimited wealth. The other mantra that I talked about earlier that is useful in this pandemic time is called Maha mrityunjaya mantra. It gives you victory over death and destroys all the negativity and all disease. And that is "tryambakam yajamahe sugandhim pushtivardhanam Urva rukamiva bandhanan mrityor mukshiya maamritat." You can get the recording or you can just repeat that mantra. The meaning of the mantra is not important, but it is the sound vibration that does the work because the whole creation is based on sound. The sounds are the building blocks of creation. It is also very important who gives the mantra because the guru or the one who gives you the sound he puts his energy behind the mantra so the mantra is already infused with his shakti. The mantra is more powerful than the atomic bomb because the mantra has nuclear power to displace the atoms from their location. Like if you have any disease or cancer or tumor and you target a mantra or sound vibration on that spot or on that condition, they will get dissolved. It will get dislodged just through the power of the sound because sound can travel in the space an infinite distance. That's why Babaji says the mantra is more powerful than the atomic bomb. The power of the mantra is infinite. It is beyond words because what it does is it disrupts your karma, stubborn karma. Karma is the thinking process or thinking pattern, whatever negativity you have acquired from your ancestors on your lineage or from previous births. Mantra even can destroy your karma. A simple mantra like Har har har har har har Shankar. We used to sing that in the ashram. Har means to remove, take it away. It takes away your karma just the sound will do that. It will take away the most stubborn karma or thinking pattern from your past lives of several lifetimes. Basically what you're doing is removing the Karma, just by using the sound. It depends on what you want to accomplish. There is a mantra for that. For example, this mantra, arakara by saint Tirumala in the south, you can do the impossible. If you say Arakara, Arakara that is an impossible buster sound. You can accomplish anything because arakara disrupts the chatter that is always going on in your mind. I think there are books written just on the sound. If you just keep on repeating, it destroys all the negativity and you can achieve the impossible.

There are longer mantras and there are seed mantras like you plant a seed of a tree and the tree grows there like a mango tree, so just like that There are seeds, sounds of the Divine Mother. We talked about that for the Goddess of Wealth. We talked about Shreem as the seed mantra for the Lakshmi. Then Kleem is clearly the mantra for the relationship and shows if you're having a problem in relationships use a Kleem mantra, and there you can find hundreds of YouTube videos and testimonies of people who are able to get a relationship they wanted. We talked about Hreem that is the mantra of the Divine Mother that pervades the entire cosmos, queen of all the galaxies.

So for mantras, science is phenomenal. But for starters, you can do Om Namah Shivay and of course, you know the hare Krishna mantra that Prabhupada made popular in the West. There are one hundred and eight centers of the ISKCON family, where thousands of people chant, Hare Krishna, hare Krishna Krishna Krishna hare, hare Ram hare Ram, Ram ram hare hare. They call it Mahamantra. There's basically the name of the Rama and the Krisna, the name removes all the negativity, suffering and sorrow. Basically, it gives you control of your mind, your mundane thoughts like 50 thoughts per minute subside, then you also get peace of mind and bliss. Also you realize the God which is inside of you. That's the power of the mantra. We'll talk more about it, but the mantras are also used in all the rituals like bathing, fire ceremony, like a daily ritual, the ritual bathing of the Lord is done with the mantra. There are mantras for invoking Him, like inviting Him over here. That means I invite you and give you a seat. Of course, in the fire ceremony, there is sacrifice and there are thousands of mantras that are repeated, depending on what is the purpose of the fire ceremony. Mantras are powerful when you receive them from a formal teacher. Mantras will give you the power to achieve, to control your mind. And by doing that, you can achieve whatever you want. After a mantra, comes the ritual. If you go to any temple, temples are basically just a center for rituals. The rituals are conducted for the entire community and the different gods are invoked in whatever temple you go to. There are thousands of temples just in one city Varanasi where I grew up. There are temples in every holy city in India known to us. Also, there are temples in all major cities in U.S.–Los Angeles, San Francisco, Atlanta, Pittsburgh, San Diego, New York, Boston, Chicago, Philadelphia.

The ritual I want to talk about is the fire ceremony because Babaji says worshiping the fire is worshiping the inner light, the Jyoti. Basically God appears in the fire and whatever you offer To the fire goes directly in the mouth of gods and goes directly to the gods in heaven. By invoking gods in heaven, inviting them to come down and take this offering and in turn, they give you whatever you request. In Geeta, Krishna says, "It's like you scratch my back, I scratch your back." It is called Parasparam in Sanskrit. You are basically Inviting gods and goddesses to the fire ceremony. I've been doing it every day at least since 2010. For example, first we invoke Ganesha with the mantra to remove all the obstacles. Then we do mantras for Brahma Vishnu Mahesh, which is the creator god, the sustainer god, and the destroyer god. Then after that, we have a mantra for the Guru or the Babaji. Then we invoke Kal Bhairav who we talked about earlier for protection. Then we have a mantra for the goddess Lakshmi for wealth, and we invoke the Durga to destroy the negativity. Then we have the mantra for Rama Vishnu, and all the nine planets and Jesus Christ. Finally, we have the final offering so you can see we invite all the gods from the heavens to come down and we feed them and in turn, they bless us as well as purify the environment. The crime rate goes down in the neighborhood and the space gets cleaned. You have the perfect place to go for meditation because your home becomes like a cathedral or a temple. So this is the power of the fire ceremony. Not only is it good for you, but also it is good for the area that you live in and for the environment. I've been doing this like once a week ever since I met Babaji and he gave me this process or this technique.

In the beginning, I used to do that twice a day, once in the morning and once in the evening, because I could not live without it as it gives you so much charge. You are just recharged with incredible power, energy and bliss. Every place I have lived since 1984 has been transformed into a holy place. Now there is a huge temple nearby where I had lived. For example, in Sunnyvale when I first came with my wife, we lived in an apartment. I used to do the morning opening ceremony, as we do, all the rituals like I was living in an ashram, living in India. As a result of that transformation that happened in the energy or vibration of this space is that it becomes very conducive to prayers, and a very peaceful environment is created. All the negativity is destroyed, all the demons are literally driven away by the Shakti. There's no negativity, so, the perfect place to build a temple. This large temple in Sunnyvale is called the Sunnyvale Hindu Temple, I believe. It's very close to where we used to live. That's just one example. Then we moved to Fremont and we lived there from 1995 to 2004 for ten years. There is a huge community developed because we used to invite people from the neighborhood, all friends and family, to do the fire ceremony followed by a wonderful feast, we used to sing and chant, with the kids and the families. It created a great community and also, the Temple in Fremont became very popular and people used to come from India. All the different saints from different parts of India heard about this Hanuman temple and they used to come in the summer almost every week. You'll have a preacher or a priest or saint come in giving you the preaching. We just transformed the entire neighborhood. Then from Fremont, we moved to the East Coast, the Boston area. I lived in Shrewsbury, and I started doing the same routine there. We built a fire pit outside called Havan Kund. We started doing the Yagya, the fire ceremony and then chanting. Japa in the morning and then all the rituals. Slowly we invited all the friends and neighbors, all the Indian community, because they are more familiar with the rituals, but we also invited people, anybody who is interested in life or elevating their consciousness for the lack of a better word for the peace and harmony and love of God. We created a great community and we lived in this development called Shrewsbury Hunt.

When the kids were grown up, we wanted to move to the west coast. While we were selling our house, all the real estate agents told us the whole community had been transformed and the real estate agents used to call it Indian Hunt, because there was so much Indian community had developed around what used to be Shrewsbury Hunt. The message here is that the power of the rituals goes beyond your individual Needs. Not only will it fulfill all your needs, but also it purifies the community and purifies the space, purifies the environment, and most importantly, affects climate change. The Yagyas is a great boon for the climate change that we are going through right now. This Yagya or fire ceremony in the Vedic tradition has been described in literature and is called Puranas and also Yajurveda. Scripture describes the very detailed process of Yagya that was used, before the birth of Rama, the avatar. The story goes that in those days people used to live several thousand years. Dashrath the king wanted a son to inherit his kingdom. He hid his age. He was like sixty thousand years old and he could not have any children, even though he had three wives who lived with him. He went to his Guru, and he looked at his birth chart and they did especially design Yagya for him so that he could have a son. So soon a very elaborate Yagya was performed. Valmiki, in Valmiki Ramayana, gives you detailed instructions on how that Yagya was performed. Shringi Rishi who was performing the Yagya got a fruit that was blessed in the fire ceremony and gave it to Dashrath. He told Dashrath to give the blessed fruit to his wife so that she can have a son. His oldest wife Kaushslya shared the fruit with his two younger wives. Kaushalya had two sons named Ram and Lakshman. The two other wives had one son each and named them Bharat and Shatrughan.

Rama himself, when he was born, played a very active role from an early age in protecting the Yagyas. Actually his Guru came to take Rama with him when he was very young and he said to his father, "I want to take Rama with me to protect my Yagya From the Demonic forces. Because the Demonic force doesn't like the Yagya, the light, and the energy in the radiance, because it destroys them so they create a lot of disturbance. It's very important to remove the negativity and purify your place before doing the Yagya. We invoke the presence of Rama and Hanuman." So from the very beginning from the time of the ancient Veda, they have been helping humanity and the gurus perform this Yagya because it transforms the hearts of people. You become a noble person and all the negativity is destroyed. Babaji did that every morning. He woke up like 3:30-4:00 am and after the bath and meditation the first thing Babaji will do is a Yagya. He had one of the fire pits built inside his small room and one outside. The first thing he would do was go outside and do a Yagya. I participated when I was in Herakhan in 1982. Babaji revived the ancient complex fire ceremony. Because if you read Valmiki Ramayana, it is a very complex process. They use different kinds of trees and herbs and there are so many combinations. He made it very simple and he gave a specific mantra and infused it with his energy and the primary goal of Babaji's Yagya is to establish peace in the world. When I came back from Herakhan in '82-'83, we used to go around the country and do Peace Yagya where we'll repeat The Shanti mantra chanting, mantra for peace. The peace mantra: Om Sahana vavatu, sahno bhunaktu, sah viryam Karva vahe. Tejaswi Navadhitamastu mavidve sa Vahe. Om Shanti Shanti Shanti

A bunch of other devotees will go with me and we will go around in a different part of the country to do The Shanti Yagya, and we'll repeat this Mantra 56 times in the fire ceremony, and it will destroy all the negativity and establish peace. That's what we need. Right now is peace or Shanti Yagya, one of the most important rituals because it not only gives you health but also gives you wealth. After I did the first Yagya at Campbell Hot Springs where Leonard orr used to live In the Sierra Nevada mountains, I went back to India and I showed Babaji the picture of the Yagya or fire ceremony in the U.S. I showed him a picture of the first Yagya that we did in Campbell Hot Springs (CHS). Leonard Orr had a place in the Sierra Nevada mountains called Campbell Hot Springs, he had six hundred sixty acres of land and he had these hot sulfur baths. He used to call them Shiva baths where people used to go and soak. We created a huge Havan Kund there where we used to do a fire ceremony up in the Sierra Nevada mountains. I took those pictures and showed them to Babaji and he said, "Oh, were you there doing this?

I said, "Yeah. I was there for sure."

He said, "If you do this Yagya, your income will double, more than double."

I started Doing Yagya whenever I could on the weekend, sometimes in the evening and my income had doubled-not only doubled but had gone up tenfold by the time I retired, almost 30 years later. So Babaji's Yagya is designed to please the Divine mother which is the proximity of mother nature. The immediate effect on the climate is seen after you perform Yagya and nature and the environment are purified. If it's a Cloudy day, then immediately the sun will come up and so the great transformation happens instantly. All the bacteria are destroyed. All the vegetation and the plants you can see thrive where the Yagyas are performed and people can feel the energy from miles.

When I lived in the Boston area, I used to invite people to my fire ceremony. One of the devotees, I remember she told me as soon as she started driving toward our home for the fire ceremony she started crying as she felt the energy was so pure. It's a great ritual and basically what happens, your home becomes a spiritual center or a home ashram, and it's called Grihastha Ashram or family Ashram. You can live and in harmony with your friends and neighbors and with your work and discover your true self, and then all your desires are fulfilled and eventually you get Moksha or liberation. You become one with the gods. That's why it is very important to do these rituals and practices and is not limited to ashrams in India and holy places. Your home will become an ashram and will become like a holy place and all the gods and goddesses will reside there like my home center. I have been doing this and the same thing can happen to you if you follow these practices and do these rituals and meditation then your home will become a holy place and all the gods and goddesses will come and reside.

So we completed the ritual section. We can see there's no end to Rituals. The most important thing is devotion and faith and then persistence like we talked about earlier. Mahendra Maharaj also talks about this– shraddha or faith as number one and number two is tolerance. Sai Baba of Shirdi also talks about Shraddha and Saburi–Shraddha means faith and Saburi means patience. You have to have faith just like Jesus said–if you have faith, you can move mountains. With faith and patience, you can achieve all your goals of life including immortality and victory over death. Everything is possible if you surrender your rational or monkey mind and devote your life to these practices.

Now we will talk about meditation. So, all the Siddhas, our perfect masters, are always engaged in meditation. I have like 500 different types of meditation. It depends on what you want to accomplish. It is one way to go deep inside and the biggest benefit of meditation is the peace of mind. Peace is the perfume of God. That means you're getting closer and closer to God. You'll experience this indescribable, just the most amazing peace that surpasses all understanding and it can be achieved through meditation. I'll walk you through the first meditation on Om Namah Shivaya. That is the mantra capable of giving you everything including the victory over death. Om Namah Shivaya. Om itself is this God or the sound that in the beginning was the Word and the Word became flesh and dwelt among us. You can realize God because Om is God. There is research by NASA on the sound of the sun. As they got closer to the sun, they recorded the subtle sound of the sun's vibration. The subtle sound is Om like its own. Now I must tell you, the five letters in the Mantra are the five elements and NA represents the Earth element which is in the lower part of your body so you can focus on your eyes and just the sound NA. Focus on your toes and feet now. Toes and the Shins and calf. You have muladhara at the base of the spine and then you move on to your stomach and the swadhisthana area that's where this water element resides and Ma represents the water element. So in toning, sending the MA sound vibration into your stomach and all the way through your chest up to the chest and this water in the sound. That controls the water element Ma. So Babaji has control over five elements through this Mantra Namah Shivaya. If you can control five elements, you can stop the earthquake with the sound NA the Earth element. Now we are at the belly button and the stomach and so you can meditate on different parts in your stomach, your gallbladder, your kidney or your intestines, your liver and you can heal any disease with the sound and the light Emanating from the mantra ma-ma-ma-ma-ma. You can keep repeating it and the sound and the light will go to the area that's most needed that has a Darkness or congested energy or disease as you call it. It will dissolve all the darkness or congestion. We are still meditating on the sound Ma. Ma represents the water element and it fills the entire area between your muladhara and your heart center. You can just intone or send sound to the area that is affected and requires attention and you can send the sound Ma and the photon energy associated with that to rearrange the atoms. The sound will work itself. All you need to do is just focus on the area of discomfort within your stomach region. We talked about the liver or if you have gallbladder or pancreas issues, if you have pancreatic cancer or diabetes you just intone or implant sound Ma and visualize Ma going from mouth into your stomach or different parts of your body. We'll do mama mama-mama going to focus on them On the stomach area, gallbladder, kidney, liver and pancreas. Now we move to the heart, chest, and physical heart and entire chest and now visualize the Fire Element.

The power of the element is again, beyond the mind because the five elements are called Pancha Bhootas that have created everything visual everything that you see in the world whether it is a human body or non-human moving or non-moving object.

Everything is created by the five elements–Pancha Bhootas and water makes 70% of the body. Now we go to the fire element, the fire, which is on in our hearts. We meditate on the chest and the heart region and I'm going to intone every cell of the chest and the heart region with the sound SHI. If you have heart disease or any condition, it will destroy all the negativity, hatred, jealousy, anger, and invoke love and compassion. Just with the sound SHI you derive joy, the bliss and the happiness by the chanting from the heart, that's what destroys all the negativity. Just feel the peace, love, and harmony. SHI the sound representing the fire element will take care of your lungs or breathing problem all the covid people who have breathing issues. I used to have a breathing problem as a child as I had asthma. I healed it just by chanting the sound SHI. VA represents the air element and that is in your throat, The thyroid gland, and there's a chakra called vishuddhi chakra this way all the thoughts are emanating, and also this chakra stores Karma, from the past life. The air element also covers the shoulders where past life karma is stored. By intoning the sound VA in your two shoulders and the throat you can diffuse past life karmas. Now, we'll just focus on the third chakra and sound. Ya, Ya. Ya, represents the ether, akash or space element and is located in the upper part of your body, your brain, your two eyes. The third eye, two ears and the crown chakra thousand petal lotus is filled with the space sound Ya. Yahweh is the sound of God in Hebrew. We'll just say Ya. Ya. The space that is outside is also inside. every pore in your body, in your ears through your nose and out through your mouth, actually the entire body. Is filled with the Ya, and with this space. When, this space inside becomes space outside you become omnipresent. You become non-local by chanting the Mantra. Ya. Ya. Ya. Ya., It improves your eyesight and improves your hearing. If you have hearing difficulty want to, improve your sense of smell and taste. you can just do Om Namah Shivaya. You can just chant Om Namah Shivaya. Loudly all night. When I met Babaji for the first time, he said one night that people should sing Om Namah Shivaya, Om Namah Shivaya all night. We used to do twenty-four hours of chanting, we just sat and chanted loudly Om Namah Shivaya. This power of this mantra of meditation on the five elements is infinite and it can heal any disease in your body. Yes, with the help of the sound, all of us, depending on what the problem is, where it is located. Just the sound will go and reconfigure all the atoms you just need to concentrate on the sound and not on any other thoughts. That is the meditation on Om Namaha Shivaya, a meditation on five different sounds. I want to give you another very powerful meditation on the light. Because light is all we are made up of. So before I do that, I want to read you something from Angela, who achieved her oneness with Christ about believing and what she said, "First, there must be the power to believe without doubting. Then that belief will grow into positive, definite knowledge. All that really matters is that you must reach the point where you will know often initially through your own testing."

Whether these things are true or not, you must never accept the word of others as your own individual testimony. If you do, then you will never have the power to live by the strength of those higher hearts. There should not be the slightest criticism. It is true that when we know the truth, then he is held accountable for the truth, and if he loves truth more than he loves life, then he's willing to die for it. You can. With the song and the like, and you will know the truth, as many people who have known the truth but have loved their own lives more than they have the truth. Now we're going to practice the glorious first great commandment, and this is a meditation on light, so as you take time out to practice the glorious first and great commandment, getting the organs of your body united and unified in a spirit of true love, eternal and divine. From here on I ask that after practicing that commandment, you begin to visualize the light pouring out from you. You will not see it at first, but you will feel it. Now, as often as you think of it, turn your attention to this inner light and with your conscious mind, send it out from you to heal and bless the world. Soon you will be able to see it with your physical eye and others will begin to feel it. When one is born of the spirit it is this great inner divine self, which in steps force into power and the literal mortal ego-self is completely put aside. The easiest way to begin to send the allied forces is to sit quietly, practicing that first and great commandment, unifying the whole body in love and then as it becomes vibrating with love. Transfer it into this light and send the light out from you. You'll feel that the very strongest rays go out from the very center of your body. But soon you will actually be radiating light from every cell of your being and those whose vibrations are not lifted high enough to see it will not see it, but yet they will feel it. You need to train yourself to hold this light constantly and to send it out with magnified power as you send out this light. You can either direct it to an individual group or just send it out and it will reach those who are in tune with it and unite with their light or help those who need healing, try to never lose consciousness of it for one moment.

This is how Christ brought it forth to accomplish his work and to fulfill his destiny. The light of Christ is joy and song and ecstasy and glory that is unspeakable as you hold onto that ecstasy, the darkness will soon be banished forever. And joy, such as you have never known, will be yours forever. You will be cleansed from all past mistakes and prepared to be filled with the light or to receive your anointing of light. Then that quickening spirit is given to abide in us. Therefore, it is up to us to bring it forward. Now, as you hold yourself in that vibration of joy and glory and praise and rejoicing, what you're really doing is holding yourself in the purifying, glorifying flame of the spirit of Almighty God, his holy spirit. This is done by your own conscious thinking as you begin to understand that it is entirely a matter of thinking or awareness of understanding and that this tremendous power to constantly contact this glorifying spirit of God or the light of Christ is right within you at all times and begin to use it with understanding. You will understand completely and forever at your own responsibility and why it is necessary to cast darkness from you. When you learn to contact that light within you and to light that light, you can ask anything and have it granted. That is such unspeakable power, such dynamic, breathtaking knowledge waiting for those who will only try to leave. Hold onto that belief, it will gradually develop into faith and vision and finally will become complete knowledge and knowledge is power. It is true that as we develop this light and love, it attracts people to us and it is only as we fully realize that it is not as they are reaching for but the light of the Christ, which they feel. That understanding is the first requisite to advance the self.

We must truly provide that God can work for us and that we give him the glory for every step of progress we make is most useful. That is a little like meditation, for you are the light that makes everything in the world, The Holy Spirit of God of meditation. Life is full of grace and love and joy. Regardless of what the name is, the light is inside of you and you can tune into it. You can draw on it. You can send it anywhere. You can heal yourself. You can heal your body. You can heal others. This is what is called the Holy Spirit or the goddess, the Divine Mother and that light makes everything. In Sanskrit, it's called Jyoti Agni. Jyoti Agni means light is fire and fire is light. Jyoti is called the goddess the Divine Mother because that's what everything is made of. You can also meditate on the seven chakras and infuse each one with the light of the goddess and who is also known as Kundalini. Kundalini is coiled like a snake that is dormant at the base of the spine. When it is awakened through sound vibration or through singing or through the company of a saint. The energy begins to rise at the base of the spine and starts penetrating each Chakra. The first one is at the base of the spine, Mula Dhara. In each chakra there is a center of Power. People meditate on, sound Lum or, gum for Ganesha at the base of the spine and then the second one is the Sex Chakra or is called Swadhistan Chakra. There is a lot of stubborn karma stored in each chakra and you can use sound and light to clear the Karma. That's the secret of chanting that the energy moves through each chakra. You can target the sound. Send it to different chakras for cleaning. In quiet meditation, you can dissolve the karma. The third chakra is at the navel. Some people meditate on Vishnu; that's when you connect it to the power of the creator Brahma.

You have seen the pictures of Vishnu with Brahma, the creator, coming out of his navel, sitting on the lotus. Some people meditate on the sound of the goddess Lakshmi Shreem. You can put different sounds or mantras on different chakras. The fourth Chakra is the heart or Anahat chakra. Anahat means unstruck sound. The heart is the seat of the soul. Of course, the heart is where the light of the self-dwells. Some people meditate on the light of the divine in their hearts. Babaji meditated on the Divine Mother haida khandeshwari that resides in her heart. There are seven hundred verses written in praise of the Divine Mother who lives in the heart. The light or the meditation on the light of the heart gives you Abhista Siddhi, to say the least, to do, to have power, abhist means whatever you want can be achieved. All the devas or shining beings and all the gods salute that goddess because this goddess rules the entire cosmos and as a sound, permeates the entire universe. You meditate on that light. You can get all of your heart's desires fulfilled–she gives you peace. This is one way to bypass the mind, rational mind and go into the heart and know and get your heart's desires fulfilled.

So from the heart chakras, we go to the throat chakra, which we talked about earlier–it's called the Vishuddhi chakra. There's a 12 Petal lotus and it's also called Neelkanth blue throat through which Shiva drank the poison, a cosmic poison. There was the churning of the ocean in the Milky Way, a nectar has generated as well a poison, so that is the story. At the beginning of the creation, there was a samudra manthan, or the churning of the milky ocean in the galaxy. There were gods on one side and demons on one side churning the ocean. When they used this huge snake called Vasuki for churning the ocean, he was spitting the poison profusely. That poison called Halahal had to be removed. Shiva at that point drank the Halahal poison and when his wife Parvati saw that, she tried to stop the poison from going down his throat by choking him. His throat became blue because of the choking. That's why Shiva is called Neelkanth, one with a blue throat.

In the cosmic space, there is a lot of poison that we have in the space inside of us. The meditation on the blue throat removes a lot of karma from the past lives that we stored in our throat space or Vishuddhi chakra. The data stored in the space is called the Akashic records. It is just like the cloud storage we use to store our digital data. The universe has been using the Akashic or space records forever to store. All of our acts, all of our karma, from our past lives, is stored in the Akashic records. All the thoughts come from the Akashic records through our throat chakra. When we express or try to articulate and are not able to express something, our throat chakra is blocked. We have to meditate on the space in the throat or blue throat to remove all your past life karma. All the negativity or stubborn thought processes from the past make an impression that can be removed by meditating on the throat space or vishuddhi chakra. Some people just sing kirtan all the time, just chant it out loud, sing it out loud, like twenty-four hours on power times like Shivaratri. We used to do that every week in the 80s when I came back from India to the Bay Area. We used to chant all night Om Namaha Shivaya. Singing clears the throat chakra and then the next chakra is called Agya chakra is the third eye, the pituitary gland is located between the two eyebrows. It's called the third eye and it does literally look like a third eye. You have seen pictures of Kali with the third eye. You can meditate on a vertical third eye. It encompasses the pituitary gland and the pineal, which is in the middle of the brain, also called the miracle brain. You can meditate on the flame or lighting in your third eye. When you see the ladies with a red dot on the third eye or the Gurus from India with a red dot between the two eyebrows they are activating their third eye.

The third eye is the one eye that Jesus talks about. It is the most powerful Chakra. It is called Agya chakra or command chakra. All other chakras follow this chakra because this is where the soul resides. That is your third eye and then on the top of our head, we have a thousand Petal lotus or crown chakra. When we meditate on Om Namah Shivay, the Shakti that resides on the bottom of the spine rises to merge with Shiva in the crown of your head. Buddha, when he achieved Nirvana, his hair became curly and all the energy basically went to the crown and all 38,000 nerves, which is close to, basically the full activation of every neuron in the brain. You can fully awaken all the different parts of the brain. It can happen through meditation or through chanting. We'll talk about the brain and sound in the next chapter. With sound different parts of the brain will get activated. The entire brain can be activated thru sound called global activation. That's a meditation on the seven Chakras. Shiva is always in meditation because all the mysteries are inside of us within us. You are the universe. There is a book about this written by Deepak Chopra called *You Are the Universe*.

You can see everything is inside that light, which is the light that shines within the heart and that's the light that shines in heaven, the highest heaven, and that's the light of the mother or the Jyoti or the Christ light and everything made of that. Nothing is hidden from you and nothing is impossible because everything is the mother. When you become one with the mother in meditation, that's how you achieve oneness with life with the mother. Eventually, you become the vast light and then you're not afraid of death. Just like Jesus, you sacrifice your body because you know, you're the light and then you can come back. Because you're not the body, you're not the mind, you're the soul, then you turn on the light that cannot be destroyed. That's indestructible. That's who you are. In meditation, you can find the self. If you have the faith and you persevere and then all the mystery is revealed to you and you'll know the truth, that you're like your God.

CHAPTER 11

Reprogramming the brain

"Solve all your problems through meditation. Exchange unprofitable religious speculations for actual God-contact. Clear your mind of dogmatic theological debris; let in the fresh healing waters of direct perception. Attune yourself to the active inner Guidance; the divine voice has the answer to every dilemma of life."

~ Lahiri Mahasaya

Reprogramming the brain to change your consciousness is something I've been working on for several years, for the last five, six years, and I had great success. First of all, understanding the brain itself, the brain is just the receiver of thoughts—it does not produce thoughts. The brain has to be activated. There are different parts of the brain that have different functions And without getting too technical. We want to just recognize that there are, mainly five parts of the brain like a frontal lobe, a right brain, left brain that most people are familiar with, the right hemisphere, left hemisphere, the back of the brain and to the top of the brain. Much of the neurons are located in the back of the reptilian brain.

The easiest way to activate the different parts of the brain, I have learned, is to add to the brain and mind their consciousnesses by a gentle touch, sound, or light. There are various ways of touching, various sounds, and lights we can use to activate the full brain. The first one is you can just turn the light on inside your brain, just visualize a flame in the third eye, which is the pineal gland, and also tap on the space between the two eyebrows where the pituitary gland is located and feel a slight pressure activating the pineal gland. Now we will go through several techniques. The first one that is very common is to use the primordial sound Om. In the beginning, was the Nada, the sound which is known as the word and the Word became flesh and dwelt among us, that sound is Om.

As you chant Om, Om, Om, it wakes up your brain, your mind, your consciousness, and also, all four states of consciousness like waking, sleeping, dreaming as well as beyond, will get activated. It will take you into the fourth state of consciousness, which is called Turia or beyond. That's why Om is part of all the Hindu prayers. The first word that is recited is Om. That's why in the morning you could just say Om three times. Om, Om, Om, and the entire brain is activated. Another song that gives you the full activation or the global activation of the brain is the Ah sound. Aum actually consists of three different sounds ah, UU and MM that's what makes all. If you cannot say the Om sound, you can just say, ah-ha. There are ah meditation available that you can use, but just ah sound. Will activate the brain. Now, another simple technique to activate the third eye and awaken the Kundalini, the prana, the lightning that moves inside the spine is a very simple tapping of the third eye that is called the midbrain miracle method. You simply tap on the space between the two eyebrows, with the finger-like pinky and slightly tap and feel, tap and feel tap and feel, it will awaken your pituitary and pineal gland in the brain and all the karmic deposits in the frontal lobe will be released. It erases your job identity, your social identity, your relationship identity. Everything you see that is deposited in the frontal lobe will be Erased by simple tapping. You see the Indian women who are married have like a little dot between the two eyebrows, the red dots. That is why they do that by just putting that dot or the bindi or the red dot, by pressing on the pituitary gland or activating the midbrain, which is the primal brain, not the cortex, not the surface brain.

Another simple technique to still the mind and to focus attention on your left eye and from there focus your attention on the right brain, because the left eye is connected to the right brain and the right eye is connected to the left brain. We want to activate the right, the creative side of the brain. We just simply focus on your left eye. The light shoots from the left eye into the right brain. The right brain lights up, so you close your eyes and do this practice or exercise. Again, we close our eyes and. Focus on the left eye and let the light fill up the right side of the brain. Now you can open your eyes and put your attention on the left nostril and then on the pituitary gland and the pineal gland because the left nostril is actually connected to your third eye or your pituitary gland.

The yogis do pranayama, which is breathing, taking breath through the left nose first, and they hold the breath and then release it from the right side of the nostril. What that does is activate the pineal and pituitary gland. You just simply breathe in through the left nostril, focus on the pituitary and the pineal gland. This technique will centralize your thoughts or atomize Your thoughts. What that does is it makes your thoughts very powerful. With this practice, you can make your thoughts powerful so that they will manifest. With this practice, you can get into the region of the brain that we are targeting in just a few minutes. Once you atomize the thought, the thought will manifest and you can think and easily manifest. This genius intelligence technique has been used from the beginning of time by the yogis. Living today we have 40 to 50 thoughts in the brain every minute. Through this technique, you focus on one thought so you can atomize the thought and manifest it. This technique you can practice with your family on the dining table in just a few minutes and focus on atomizing thoughts and see the beauty and radiance in the universe that's already there. But because of our monkey mind, we don't see the beauty of the universe. We only see the surface. So by activating the inner eyes or the third eye, you are able to see the beauty and radiance or they call it God. Everywhere.

Another technique is to infuse the five senses, two eyes, two ears, two nostrils, mouth, and brain with different sounds to create clarity and more light in the brain. This technique, the way it works, is through controlling the five senses. As most of the input to the mind is through the five senses, a disturbed mind has a lot of contradictory and confusing, overwhelming inputs unconsciously through our senses. By controlling the five senses by fusing with the light or sound, we are changing our perception, by seeing the maya or creation through different prescription glasses. You start seeing everything with a lot more clarity, with more insight by using this technique of controlling the input to the five senses. It is actually a technology where you close your eye and first focus on the left eye and fill it with a bright light, very bright light. Then you focus on the right eye and fill it with the bright light. Then focus on your left nostril, and again the light goes into your left nostrils to the pituitary gland and then repeat the process with the right nostril. Then you fill in your mouth with the bright light and go to the tonsils and you can fill up your whole body with the light. With this technique, you focus on the two ears and you fill up with the light. The left ear and right ear and then the brain, you fill up the brain with the light, descending from the heavens filling up your entire body, the brain first and the whole brain gets activated and filled with light. You've become a Deva or a shining being, and every part all the way from the top of your head to the tip of your toes gets filled up with light. You can start now, go to the top of your head and fill up your entire body with the light. You become the light. That's the technique that yogis use to turn their bodies into the light. Basically what you're doing is you're getting into higher consciousness from lower consciousness, from the physical realm to heaven, to the realm of light and the spirit and becoming one. Then there are people who have spent their lifetime just practicing with this technique. That's how they turned their body into light and there are several saints in the south.

There was a saint called Swamy Ramalingam, who turned his body into light and of course, in the north 500 years ago, there was Kabir Saheb. I'm sure a lot of people have heard of Kabir and there's a huge following that he turned his body into light. There was Mira and there is Jesus, who used the same technique to turn his body into light, and so the technique is very simple, but it just requires a lot of practice. Through practice, you can not only heal your body parts any disease, anywhere in the body, and eventually you can turn the body into the light. Just like what Paul said, "With the blink of an eye, you can turn the body into light." That is a very powerful meditation. It starts with the brain because the brain is a receiver of the thoughts, but it can also be the receiver of the light. There are techniques like the sun and moon, eclipse meditation to activate the miracle brain and the heart to be free from the Maya or the illusion because everything we see is not real. What you see is a delusion or Einstein used to call it persistent illusion. Everything is an illusion. Everything is energy. It just takes different forms and different shapes to delude us and to get free from that is to do a sun-moon eclipse meditation that I will walk you through to activate the miracle brain.

In the heart, to be free from the Maya, the way it works is that you close your eyes and visualize the sun in your left hemisphere and full moon in your right hemisphere and slowly the Moon starts traveling towards the sun in 16 steps like phases of the moon. You can visualize the sun and then slowly bring in the light of the moon or the moon from the right side of the brain slowly traveling towards the sun and slowly taking over the sun like an eclipse. Then slowly take over the entire sun, such that you just see a light ring right around the sun like a diamond ring. You only see the light emanating from one point around the sun. You fill up your mind with that. With that light you can do the same sun-moon meditation in your heart. Now you can put a bigger flame into your heart, like a picture of Jesus with light or with a lamp in his heart so you can light up that lamp and bring the light much bigger than the third eye. Start with the sun filling up your physical heart and then Your chest and then you bring in the moon, the full moon slowly filling up the entire heart space. Then slowly the moon with its 16 phases starts covering the sun. The radiance of the sun becomes more pleasant, more soothing and we can count slowly from 1,2, 3, 4, 5, 6, 7, 8, 9, 10, 11, 12, 13, 14, 15, 16, the full moon covers the sun in your heart. Again, there is a ring all around the sun, like an eclipse. You can add different colors to the light, like a sunset. You can see orange, red, vermilion, and pink colors but it's more like the colors of the rising sun, but only in a ring and around the ring which looks like a huge diamond ring that is glittering from the sun. You fill up your heart with that light and that's the same light that shines in everyone. Soon after you practice this meditation, then you only train your mind to see that light. If anyone you meet and your mind and heart will be changed just to see the light or the Divine Mother because that's the light that creates everything visible, non-visible. In the lotus of the heart, you can see a rising sun. With this meditation when you practice, you'll be able to gain victory over Maya or you will be in control and you will not be affected by up and down. The happiness, sorrow, victory, defeat, loss, and the gain would have no effect on you. It will be the same for you because you see light in everything. It is a very powerful meditation. And just like in any other meditation, people spend their lifetime practicing this. You can start slowly. That's how you are not affected by Maya or up and down in life.

We talked about the sun-moon eclipse meditation, and then there's blue light meditation. The light pervades the entire body, so you can also use the blue light meditation on the throat chakra. That's where most of the karma from the past life is accumulated. That's where you have a stubborn Karma like a scarcity consciousness and low intelligence. They're all in the third chakra. There are a couple of mantras that are practiced by Shiva Babaji and his followers and the sound you can use like the breeze sound or Thiru Neela Kantam. But the trick is to visualize bright blue light piercing your throat chakra and erasing all the karmic deposits from millions of lifetimes that we have lived as it's Vishuddhi Chakra that channels all the thoughts. Meditation on the blue light and Thiru Neela Kantam sound basically purifies or removes all your scarcity consciousness that puts any limitation on your abundance, or bad relationship, or health. That is the blue light meditation on the throat. You need a guide or a place where you can do it without being interrupted regularly, at the same time, hopefully in the same place. Any time when you can, and here is how you can listen to this recording and just practice the blue light meditation on the throat and visualize all the poison being eliminated. All the darkness, which is based on the toxicity, turns into nectar. By this technique called Neelkanth, Neelkantham, or Blue Light Meditation, you can change your destiny. It will change your life as you meditate on the blue light in the third chakra, because you create your world with your words and with your thoughts and as thoughts, improve you'll have a great transformation and you'll be able to easily manifest your thoughts.

The key to all this technique is the practice and there is a saying in Hindi, Tulsidas said that almost 500 years ago, "Karat, Karat, abhyas ke jadmati Hot Sujana." By doing regular practice, even a very dull mind becomes very sharp. Because you are a diamond in the rough, you are polishing the diamond and that is your brain and you're the light. You are activating neurons and firing trillions of neurons. You become like a child. In the Bible, it says in the Ministry of Angels you continue in patience until you are perfected, so all the scriptures say the same thing. You need to continue your practice until you're perfect because God made man in his own image. We don't feel that because we don't practice. That's why some of these techniques will help you practice so that you can become perfect and become one with God.

CHAPTER 12

Wake up latent dormant energies within

"Misery nourishes ego, and happiness is basically a state of egolessness. That is the problem, the very crux of the problem. That's why people find it very difficult to be happy." ~ Osho.

"Be happy. This is an order and blessing." ~ Babaji

"Don't depend on death to liberate you from your imperfections. You are exactly the same after death as you were before. Nothing changes; you only give up your body. If you are a thief or a liar or a cheater before death, you don't become an angel merely by dying. If such were possible, then let us all go and jump in the ocean now and become angels at once! Whatever you have made of yourself thus far, so will you be hereafter. And when you reincarnate, you will bring that same nature with you. To change, you have to make the effort. This world is the place to do it."

~ Swami Paramahansa Yogananda

We can develop latent dormant energies within through meditation On the Christ light within. **"Be Perfect, even as your father, which is in heaven, is perfect"** -Matthew 5:43.

Another quote from the Bible is, "***Pray with all energy of the heart to be filled with the pure love of Christ, that when he says a prayer, we shall be purified as he is pure.***" -Moroni 7:48

The way we develop the little dormant energy within is to understand the very subtle nature of who we are beyond the body and the mind. We are the soul and the soul dwells in the body in a very subtle form and that is you. When we start practicing meditation, kundalini, yoga or Hatha yoga, or any type of spiritual practice, what happens to the dormant energies within? Through singing or chanting or praying, the light, the sound enters your body, Like when I was growing up in India in Varanasi in the house that was right next to the most sacred temple where there are five services every day for the last 500, 600 years. The mind, body, and soul get filled with this energy of sound and light. You cannot think anything else because there are hundreds and sometimes thousands of people there singing, chanting, invoking the gods. Through that energy of sound and light, God enters your body, your mind, and your soul. You basically are filled with his energy, the holy spirit and become one with him.

The dormant energies within can be activated and do get activated, and that's the way of the yogis. There are three channels of energy within your body called Ida, Pingala, and Sushumna. There is a left channel and there is a channel in the right and the middle of your spine the central channel. You can visualize a bright red laser beam piercing all your chakras, but just visualize your spinal column and there's a light. When you go to church for services or temple or even in a concert where people are singing and dancing, you already feel your body is filled with this energy. Sushumna in the spinal column is the main place for the central energy called Kundalini in Sanskrit, to travel which lies dormant at the base of the spine, like there's a light that travels and shoots up through the brain, into the sky.

There are seven central centers called chakras that get pierced and activated through the process. The first one is called Muladhara, which is located at the base of the spine and you visualize that chakra with a different sound and light. Some people visualize Ganesha, who has a potbelly and has a trunk of an elephant and has four arms and is red in color. Some people visualize that inside the base of the spine, there's an energy center, that's where you visualize a coiled serpent sitting there, which is dormant, and is not awakened. But with this sound and through this practice the energy which is dormant at the base of the spine gets awakened. That's called Kundalini, and it rises through the spine to the top of your head. You can feel the energy up on top of the head and there you connect with the energy of the universe or the cosmos, so you're no longer an isolated human being but someone connected with the energy of the cosmos.

These chakras, the literal translation of which is just a wheel, you can visualize it like a spinning wheel of energy at each of these energy centers. Normal people are not awake in their chakras or the energy centers. Their fields are dormant and when you see the lotus flower in the chakras, which is closed but when it is awakened, it blooms and has several petals.

After the muladhara, the second chakra is the Swadhisthana chakra. There is a lot of past life, karma stored in this chakra and there are meditations available for each of these chakras where all the past Samskaras are stored. What happens to energy gets stuck in certain chakras. You're not able to move your energy higher, so you always operate from the lower chakras. Through this meditation on the second chakra, that's where most people are stuck, the energy is released. People meditate on Lord Muruga in the second chakra. Muruga is another name for Kartikeya and is also his brother of Ganesha. He's also the son of Goddess Parvati and has six heads. Muruga energy is what releases the store past karma in the second Chakra. If you meditate on Muruga he is sitting on a peacock and has a brilliant golden Energy. He carries a lance, which is like a weapon, like a lightning rod in his hand. Visualize that golden lightning rod penetrates the second chakra and your whole spinal column is lit up. It releases the energy from the second chakra.

The third chakra is called navel chakra. You probably have seen that there are pictures of Vishnu on a waterbed made of the snake in the Milky Way. You visualize Vishnu on a snake bed which is in the middle of the milky ocean and from his navel there's a branch emerging on which the Brahma, the creator, is sitting. All the creative power comes through the navel chakra or Manipura.

In the navel chakra, there's a subtle connection to the Milky Way. All the energies of the universe come into your entire body through the navel chakra. It is the space where Lakshmi, the goddess, resides with Vishnu, the God of plenty and prosperity. You visualize the sound Shreeem on navel chakra. You can start visualizing this chakra spinning clockwise and it gets bigger and bigger and bigger as you meditate on your navel chakra. People spend years meditating on each chakra because it is almost like a city, and you can fill it up with the energy of the cosmos from the Milky Way. Some yogis in deep meditation meditate on the navel chakra for all the Shakti and the power. That's also a power chakra called solar plexus.

The fourth chakra on top of that is where our hearts are. It is called the Anahat chakra or the chakra of the unstuck sound. The soul resides in your heart, and that is indestructible. You are an immortal being and your soul resides in your heart into this chakra. When you sit quietly in meditation, you hear this sound that is radiating from your heart and people visualize the goddess of light in their hearts. We talked about this earlier in another chapter. Babaji visualized the Divine Mother that lives there as jyothirmayi Jagdishi or bright radiant mother of the universe that's where unconditional love resides in all the great masters. That's why you see in Jesus' heart, there's a light or flame. You'll see Jesus has a huge flame. That is the light of the mother, also this heart of infinite love, unconditional love. That's the heart chakra which emanates the unstruck sound. The sound is just what we're made of. That's the word. In the beginning, was the word and the Word became flesh and dwelt among us. Once you decide to look into your heart, you can visualize a goddess and mother into your heart.

Between the heart and the third eye in the throat chakra or the vishuddhi chakra which is 12 petal lotus blue in color and reservoir of past life karmas. By meditating on the blue light at the throat chakra and various sounds, congested energy from the past lives is diffused from Adam's apple. We have already discussed at great length the thiru neela kantam mantra in previous chapters.

The next chakra is the third eye which is located between the two eyebrows called the pituitary and the pineal gland. This is also called Ajna chakra or the command center as all other chakras follow the command of Ajna chakra, the seat of the soul. We already talked about what gives you focus and then on top of that is the thousand petal lotus which is in the crown chakra on top of your head. I just wanted to briefly go over this chakra that your body is made of.

We need to talk about the five sheaths or five Koshas. Your body is actually made up of five different bodies. The first one is called Anna Maya Kosha, which is the food body. That's the body that you see. These subtle bodies surround your food body, the next one is the gyan maya kosha which is like the body of knowledge, and there's a vigyan maya Kosha, or wisdom body. Then there is Pran maya Kosha where the Pranas or the vital forces reside, Anand Maya Kosha is the bliss body where the soul resides. These are the five types of air or the life force that runs through your body–the prana is in the heart. Apana is in the anus. The Udana is in the stomach. Vyana in the throat and Saman all over the body. So when you go into Pran maya Kosha, you're filled with this incredible energy or prana, which is the life force, and you're able to lift very heavy weights easily, like as a feather. That's how you see Hanuman carrying a mountain or Krishna lifting a hill govardhan on his pinky. They do that because of the prana maya kosha through their prana. Through their lifeforce they're able to lift the mountain. On top of that is the Anandamaya Kosha or the bliss body and that's the highest. We are made of bliss. We're not just made of flesh and blood, but made of these subtle bodies.

I just want to introduce you so that you understand and through meditation, you will be able to experience your own subtle bodies. When you get into the blissful body, you will experience the bliss. You will experience the nectar, which is a chemical that secretes from the palate called DMT, and you'll be able to experience the bliss. It's one thing to understand and to know intellectually, and another thing to experience this through meditation and with the help of a teacher or somebody who's been there. You can experience the Anandamaya kosha or the bliss body, that is the body that is eternal, that is your true nature, because you are immortal. All the Mahatmas or great souls enlightened beings add Ananda to their names like Nityananda, Yogananda, Muktananda, and Premananda, which means they have achieved that ananda or the bliss. They have found it within themselves through the practice by stopping the mind and just focusing on the divine within and also actually without. Basically they become one with the ananda that has no beginning, no end. That is why we talked about it. The five different Koshas or sheets are five different types of bodies that are made up, but we're not aware because we're so focused just on the physical or the flesh or the meat body. Then there are four different states of consciousness, which is the waking state, sleeping state, dreaming state, and then the fourth estate is the Turia or the beyond in that state, you have transcended all three states of consciousness. You hear a sound hum, um, like an Om sound, and in that state, you can think and manifest anything. All the saints, enlightened beings live in that state of consciousness. There are different techniques available for removing the deep karmic baggage of a past life from the seven chakras.

Again, we briefly touched on this sound. The different sounds you can use. You can start with Om first, but then there are other sounds we talked about, like Namah Shivaya or HariOm. When you meet a teacher, he will see which of your chakras need to be cleaned and have past lives karmas stored, and you can remove the deep karmic baggage by just going to each chakra, visualizing it, and just bombarding it with different sound frequencies. You can be free from the past, karmic bondage. What it is, is the way of thinking a thought process you have, which is coming from your past life and you're not aware of it and you're not able to change it. But by going through the different chakras, using different sounds or different visualization. You can visualize all the chakras when they're open. They're spinning. Then you are vibrant, you're full of energy. The simplest meditation for the seventh chakra is you can visualize white light on top of your crown and it's trickling down into your seven chakras on your spine. The first one is on the topmost. The seven chakras are filled with seven colors. The first one is crown chakra filled with a violet color. Then you can visualize that chakra lotus with the violet and then you come down to the third eye and that is filled with indigo color. Then you come down to your throat chakra and then fill that with the blue light, and then you come to the heart chakra and fill that with green energy and then yellow into your navel chakra. You can visualize a yellow color or something like yellow color lotus and then orange into your Sex chakra and then red in your root chakra. It is a very simple technique to first get in touch with the seventh chakra and clean them and fill them with the seven colors of the rainbow, starting with violet in the crown chakra and then indigo into your third eye and then blue chakra into the throat, green into your heart, and then yellow into a navel, orange into your sex, red into your root chakras.

Then you can add a different sound. You can experiment with different sound frequencies. Basically, you're bombarding when you feel the flow of energy is restricted or blocked, and with certain chakra, you can go to that chakra and release the flood of light. The chakra where the flow is stopped bring restricted through our past life karmas or even in this life, and so slowly as you become aware of the energy that's not moving, you can focus on it and release it and be filled with the divine light and energy from the cosmos, from the Milky Way. Basically, this karma bondage is responsible for your birth-death. All these can be eliminated. You can remove the illusion of death, sickness, old age by this mantra. So the wheel of darkness that is surrounding you is surrounding this chakra, needs to be clarified and needs to be cleaned, and by cleansing those in deep meditation, you can root out an illusion of death. Because we all are immortal souls, we have no beginning, no end, we just take on this body, but then we think that body is who we are and the body is going to die. We spend all our life trying to protect the body. But there is nothing that is just an illusion because death is the end of the body which is made of five elements. Through the meditation and Om Namah Shivaya, the mantra that is the cure for the mind, for the sickness, old age, and by asking Shiva to bless us through the mantra "Mrityunjaya Mahadeva trahimam sarnagatam janma mrityu jarayu adi piditam karam bandhne." I pray to the one who has victory over death Mahadeva, the greatest of all, God, I surrender to you, please remove all the karma that's causing my death, old age, and suffering.

Karma again is the bondage. We are an eternal, immortal being. We are Shiva. We have no birth, no deaths. We were there before we were born and we'll be there after we die, so that consciousness is achieved through Shiva by becoming one with Shiva, by praying to Shiva through this mantra will give you that consciousness. Constant repetition of the mantra called Mahamrityunjaya Mantra, mrityunjaya Mahadeva I fully surrender to you. Please remove the karmic bondage responsible for birth-death. So nurturing knowing and developing the indestructible soul is required. There are two to three mantras that say. "Shivo hum, Shivo hum, I'm Shiva, Shivo hum, Shivo hum, I am Shiva. I am Shiva." So what it boils down to is knowing who you are, which is your true self, which Has no beginning, no end, you are your soul, you're indestructible. You've taken on this body to fulfill your desires, your karma, just like you take on a role, as a doctor or an engineer, but you're not that, are you? Taking on roles in a movie as a father or mother is whatever, but you are not that right, you're just an actor, so we are playing this role, but we are immortal soul Shiva. Who has been described in Shiva Purana a text, a scripture that tells you how to please Shiva and fulfill all your desires and realize the God within us. The result of that is you realize the bliss that you are God and all the mystery will be revealed to you. You will not be affected by weather, day-to-day lows and highs, and pandemics. I will add here another quote from yoga vashisth in which Vashista, the great teacher, is teaching Rama the Avatar about life, but the reality show just continues. This is in chapter Six of Devpuja, and we're talking about Puja or worship. Vashista says, "Oh Ram, the Unreal Jeeva perceives the unreal word on account of the unreal influences of the unreality in all.

This is what can be considered as real and what isn't real and imaginary objectivity is imaginatively described by someone and the one understands one's imagination and imagines that he understands it just as liquidity in the liquid motion invent an emptiness in this space. Even so, is the omnipresence in the soul? So from the time the Lord instructed me, I have been performing the worship of the infinite selves. By the grace of such worship, though I am constantly engaged in various activities, I am free from sorrow. I perform the worship of the self who is undivided, true, apparently divided with the flowers of whatever comes to me naturally and whatever actions are natural to me to come into relationships. To possess and to be possessed is common to all embodied beings, but the yogis are forever vigilant. With such vigilance is the worship of the self. Adopting this inner attitude and with a mind utterly devoid of any attachment, I roam in this dreadful forest of sansara or the world appearance. If you do so, you will not suffer. When great sorrow, like the loss of wealth and relationship and you inquire into the nature of truth in the manner described, you will not be affected by joy or sorrow. You know how all these things arise and how they cease.

You also know the fate of the man who is deluded by them, who does not inquire into their real nature. They do not belong to you. You do not belong to them. Such is the unreal nature of the world. Do not create drama. You are pure consciousness, which is not affected by the illusory perception of the diversity in creation. If you see this, how will notions of the desirable and desirable arise, you realize this forum remains established in that area are the transcendental state of consciousness. So that sums it up. You have to make the worship of the infinite selves as part of your life and established in that area are the whole state of consciousness. Then you will not be affected by the loss and gain. So. After listening to the drama, Rama tells his teacher, my intelligence has now been purified. Now I'm free from the dirt of duality, I have realized that all this is indeed a romance. I do not desire heaven, nor do I desire dread to hope. I remain established in the self, by your grace, O Lord. I have crossed the ocean of samsara, the world experience. I have realized the fullness of direct self-knowledge. That is what our goal of life is, to have direct self-knowledge or discover our true selves. Through this practice, as we discussed, through worship and meditation, you can also be established in direct self-knowledge or discover your true self.

I'd like to conclude this chapter with a quote from the Bible that says,[1] "Let this mind be in you, which was also in Christ Jesus. Who, being in the form of God, thought it not robbery to be equal with God." So a lot of people think, if you say that I'm God, you know, it's blasphemy. But Jesus says I will say that is not robbery, To be equal with God because everybody was made in the image of God. To achieve that fourth state, consciousness, you need to develop a practice in mindset and lifestyle that leads to the joy of the self. That's where the worship of the self comes into the picture. I have developed this over 40 years and you can attend daily, weekly, monthly prayers and meditation and discourses to develop self-awareness and socialization. Liberation, that you are equal with God, that you are created in the image of God and most people are not aware of that, even if they are aware of that, they don't live and operate from that state of consciousness. That's how you can develop supernatural powers and liberation of this soul through the removal of karmic baggage, you can develop powers for living a miraculous life. You can develop abundant energy, omnipresence, and omniscience at any age, regardless of how old you are. You can nurture the relationship with the divine living in your heart, and achieve forever lasting inner peace and liberation. If you work hard, have faith, and put in the work, anything is possible because everything is within our consciousness. The Indian rishis were so generous that they gave yoga as a gift to the world. When Prime Minister Modi visited the U.S. and he gave a speech to the Senate and Congress, he said that Indian yogis were so generous they did not have a copyright on yoga, that yoga is a technology that gives you the highest intelligence, yoga is a science of concentration. The total concentration on the object is yoga. Only the self exists.

---

[1] Philippians 2:5-6

There is no object at all. Yoga is called "Chitta Vritti nirodha" in the Yoga Sutra of Patanjali, we have to stop the mind, the expansion of the mind which is called Vritti in Sanskrit. Then the self or the supernormal powers that are hidden under the mind are revealed just by repeating the words like Chitta or chitta Vritti Nirodha, or just chitt. Just by repeating that word, chitt, you can stop the mind and why you have to stop the mind, because the real self, the true self is hidden by the veil of multiple, multiple layers and layers of thoughts, you have to just peel different layers of mind and you have to keep peeling your thoughts by stopping the thoughts. When you're able to get to the bottom of it then that's where you find yourself. There's a popular poem in India that tells the newlywed bride to remove the veil so that you can see your lover. It says, "Ghunghat ke pat khol re, tohe piya milenge." Remove that veil because all the brides have this long veil and they hide. They want to see their husband or newlywed husband or lovers and can see him by removing that veil.

The point here is to remove that veil of ignorance and stupid thoughts. Then you can discover your true self, God, superintelligence, and supernormal, miraculous power that all are within yourself. That's why you remove the veil, through this practice of worship and loving God and It is very possible.[2] "Beloved, now are we the sons of God, and it doth not yet appear what we shall be: but we know that, when he shall appear, we shall be like him; for we shall see him as he is. And every man that hath this hope in him purifieth himself, even as he is pure."

Amen.

---

[2] John 3:2-3

THANK YOU FOR READING MY BOOK!

DOWNLOAD YOUR FREE GIFTS

Read This First

Just to say thanks for buying and reading my book, I would like to give you a few free bonus gifts, no strings attached!

To Download Now, Visit:
www.DiscoverYourTrueSelfBook.com/Freegift

I appreciate your interest in my book, and I value your feedback as it helps me improve future versions of this book. I would appreciate it if you could leave your invaluable review on Amazon.com with your feedback. Thank you!

www.ingramcontent.com/pod-product-compliance
Lightning Source LLC
Chambersburg PA
CBHW051127160426
43195CB00014B/2379